JOHH HOWARD
YODER

MODERN SPIRITUAL MASTERS SERIES

JOHH HOWARD YODER

Essential Writings

Selected with an Introduction by

PAUL MARTENS
AND
JENNY HOWELL

ORBIS BOOKS

Maryknoll, New York 10545

Founded in 1970, Orbis Books endeavors to publish works that enlighten the mind, nourish the spirit, and challenge the conscience. The publishing arm of the Maryknoll Fathers and Brothers, Orbis seeks to explore the global dimensions of the Christian faith and mission, to invite dialogue with diverse cultures and religious traditions, and to serve the cause of reconciliation and peace. The books published reflect the views of their authors and do not represent the official position of the Maryknoll Society. To learn more about Maryknoll and Orbis Books, please visit our website at www.maryknollsociety.org.

Published by Orbis Books, Box 302, Maryknoll, NY 10545-0302.

Queries regarding rights and permissions should be addressed to:
Orbis Books, P.O. Box 302, Maryknoll, NY 10545-0302.

Manufactured in the United States of America.

Library of Congress Cataloging-in-Publication Data
Yoder, John Howard.
      Spiritual writings / John Howard Yoder ; selected with an introduction by
Paul Martens and Jenny Howell.
      p.   cm. – (Modern spiritual masters series)
      Includes bibliographical references.
      ISBN 978-1-57075-935-2 (pbk.)
      1. Theology. 2. Spiritual life – Mennonites.   I. Martens, Paul.   II. Howell,
Jenny.   III. Title.
BX8143.Y59A25 2011
248.4'897 – dc22   2011005651

Before it is a social strategy,
nonviolence is a moral commitment;
before it is a moral commitment,
it is a distinctive spirituality.
It presupposes and fosters a distinctive way of seeing
oneself and one's neighbor under God.
That "way of seeing" is more like prayer
than it is like shrewd social strategy,
although it is both.
It is more a faith than a theory,
although it is both.

—John Howard Yoder

Contents

Acknowledgments

Grateful acknowledgment is made to the following for permission to reprint copyrighted works by John Howard Yoder: Brazos Press, a division of Baker Publishing Group, for selections from *Christian Attitudes to War, Peace, and Revolution,* ed. Theodore J. Koontz and Andy Alexis Baker, © 2009; *Preface to Theology,* ed. Stanley Hauerwas and Alex Sider, © 2002; *The War of the Lamb*, ed. Glen Stassen, Mark Thiessen Nation, and Matt Hamsher, © 2009; Baylor University Press for selections from *Nonviolence: A Brief History,* ed. Paul Martens, Matthew Porter, and Myles Werntz,© 2010; Herald Press, Scottdale PA 15683, for selections from *Body Politics* (© 1992); *The Christian Witness to the State* (© 1997); *Discipleship as Political Responsibility* (© 2003); *The Ecumenical Movement and the Faithful Church* (© 1958); *He Came Preaching Peace* © 1985); *The Jewish-Christian Schism Revisited* (© 2009); *Nevertheless* (© 1992); *The Original Revolution* (© 2003); *The Royal Priesthood* (© 1994); *What Would You Do?*(© 1992); The University of Notre Dame Press, Notre Dame, IN 45665 for selections from *The Priestly Kingdom* (© 1984); Roman & Littlefield, for excerpts from "On Christian Unity," in the journal *Pro Ecclesia* 9, no. 2 (2000); Wipf and Stock Publishers for selections from *To Hear the Word* (© 2001) and *When War Is Unjust* (© 1996); Wm. B. Eerdmans Publishing Co., Grand Rapids, MI, for selections from *For the Nations* (© 1997) and *The Politics of Jesus* (© 1994). All rights reserved. All selections used with permission. Thanks also to the journals *Pro Ecclesia* and *Concern* and to the John Howard Yoder Estate for permission to reprint additional material by John Howard Yoder.

Introduction

John Howard Yoder's biography is not especially auspicious. He grew up in the humble surroundings of a small ethnic community in rural Ohio. In his later life, he was a quiet man, a socially awkward man who made no effort to ingratiate himself with others. Many considered his disposition prophetic (for good or for ill!). He was not a martyr, nor was he an activist of any renown. For many years, he was simply a professor. Yet there is no denying that he has had a profound effect on the latter half of the twentieth century, both in terms of the academic study of theological ethics and in terms of the ecumenical practice of nonviolence.

Unfortunately, amid the attention paid to Yoder's ethics — particularly his nonviolence — the rich theological vision that both grounds and frames his ethics is frequently missed or passed over in silence. The purpose of this volume is to illuminate and give voice to Yoder's distinctive spirituality, which fosters, as the epigraph indicates, "a distinctive way of seeing oneself and one's neighbor under God." As you read through this text, we hope that you too come to the conclusion that Yoder is worthy of inclusion among the pantheon of modern spiritual masters who have given their entire existence to living and articulating a religious vision of suffering love.

A Rather Ordinary Life

As indicated above, Yoder's early years were rather ordinary by most counts. He was born on December 29, 1927, in Smithville, Ohio. In the ensuing years, he grew up attending Oak Grove Mennonite Church, where his father, great-grandfather, and great-great grandfather were active leaders for over a hundred years of the church's life.[1] In this close-knit community Yoder grew up in a religious tradition that understood both love of neighbor and nonviolence as the means by which one imitates the life of Jesus. Oak Grove was a highly educated community, and this provided Yoder with the opportunity to gain both a broad perspective on the world and a sympathetic respect for the idiosyncrasies of his own Mennonite cultural tradition. Years later he would reflect:

> I grew up in a relaxed relationship to that culture, never needing, as many do, to prove my independence of it. Never sensing any coercion to stay within it. So that my choice to stay within it, although predisposed obviously by generations of ethnic continuity and by the church faithfulness of my parents, was by no means a matter of bowing to superior pressure but was rather a willing choice made in small stages in young adulthood.[2]

From an early age, it was clear that Yoder was gifted with sharp analytical and critical abilities. In school, he excelled in writing, speaking, and music; he participated in his school's debate team, played the French horn, and had a clear bass and tenor voice that landed him the lead roles in his high school operettas. On graduation from high school, Yoder wanted to attend either the University of Chicago or St. John's College in Annapolis to study in their respective Great Books programs. As one might expect, Yoder was accepted and offered scholarships in both programs, yet out of respect for his parents' desire that he attend a Mennonite college, he attended Goshen College in Goshen, Indiana. By this point in his life, Yoder's professors and peers were certainly becoming aware of his unique intellectual gifts as he graduated with a B.A in Bible from Goshen College in just two years.

Of course, Yoder gained more than an education while at Goshen; he gained several mentors who would challenge him for many years to come. Perhaps the most important of these was Harold Bender, a most dynamic personality in his own right. Among a long list of denominational and academic leadership roles, Bender is known for his profoundly influential historical summary of the genius of sixteenth-century Anabaptism in his *The Anabaptist Vision*.[3] According to Yoder, it was Bender who instigated his own interest in Anabaptism, provided theological guidance, and pushed him into his experience with the Mennonite Central Committee (MCC) in France.

This experience with MCC, a relief agency of the Mennonite Church, began in April 1949 when Yoder was merely twenty-one years old. Leaving all of the securities of home, he moved to Valdoie, France, and into the rubble and ravages left at the conclusion of World War II. During his first years in Europe, Yoder's daily work consisted of tending to and overseeing first one, and then two children's homes. Traveling the roads of eastern and northeastern France, Yoder worked diligently to provide both food and housing to orphaned or stranded children.

Alongside these relief responsibilities, Yoder and a French pastor by the name of Pierre Widmer were asked to help the French Mennonites, left devastated by World War II, to recover their nonresistant Mennonite heritage. This he engaged eagerly, patiently building relationships with families by listening to their stories of what it was like to live under the Nazi regime. While he heard of the sacrifices many of the Mennonites had made on behalf of their pacifist convictions, he also heard of their failures and subsequent sense of shame. Living among the French Mennonites and becoming fluent in their language, Yoder, even at such a young age, served as both mentor and friend, compelling and encouraging them to reclaim their pacifist convictions.

The years in France allowed for activities outside of work too, as Yoder became interested in one of the young French Mennonites, Anne Marie Guth, whom he met while she was working in one of the children's homes. On July 12, 1952, they were married, and between 1953 and 1969 Anne gave birth to seven children, six of whom survived infancy. Yoder's marriage to Anne also kept him personally connected to the pains of war, as Anne's family suffered considerably during the war. (Her father spent over a year in Buchenwald concentration camp because his son refused to join the German army.)

As Yoder's stay in Europe continued, his intellectual ambitions also expanded. One expression of his intellectual restlessness was his pursuit of further studies at the University of Basel, where he obtained his doctorate in theology in 1957. In this context, he also studied with Walter Baumgartner, Karl Jaspers, Oscar Cullmann, and Karl Barth, the latter two leaving a prominent and lasting impression on Yoder's thought. His dissertation, however, was written in Anabaptist history under Ernst Staehelin. The dissertation, foreshadowing so much of what he would later develop, examined the debates between the Magisterial Reformers and the Anabaptists in Switzerland held in the years 1523–1538 and displayed the reasons why the Anabaptists remained faithful to the Christianity of the New Testament until the end. Despite exhibiting his usual self-confidence in this new academic arena, Yoder remained unsure about his place within it. He did not seem to understand himself as a theologian and, in correspondence with Bender as he embarked on his doctoral studies, he wrote, "From an Anabaptist point of view, I'm not sure theology is worth that much... and three more years, even though enjoyable, would hardly be justifiable if I don't plan to be a theologian, which I don't."[4]

Bender responded sharply:

> The trouble is that you are one anyway. You always have been one and you always will be. The only question is what kind of a theologian you want to be. You do not have to be a theologian of the type of any particular school of thought, but among the very few men who have endowments and attitudes which enable them to be the real theologians we need, you are one."[5]

Bender still had some influence in Yoder's life, and Yoder finished the degree.

While studying in Basel, Yoder also oversaw the Mennonite Board of Missions and Charities relief program, which originated as a response to the earthquake that ravaged Algeria in 1954. In this post, Yoder wrote a series of articles about his experiences in Algeria, Islam, war, and the relief efforts while he also participated in ecumenical conversations about pacifism. While many of these conversations occurred within the context of conferences, other conversations were held less formally, and some were even held in secret. Seemingly untiring, Yoder was also a member of the Europe Council of the International Fellowship of Reconciliation and the ecumenical committee of the German Protestant *Kirchentag* during his years in Europe.

A second, less formal expression of Yoder's intellectual restlessness emerged alongside his study at the University of Basel. In the mid-1950s, a group of North American Mennonite men working in Europe began to gather occasionally to hold informal seminars on matters of shared concern, which is to say concerns that emerged out of the difficulty these men had in translating the theological and cultural convictions they brought with them into the new contexts and questions that faced them in the ashes of postwar Europe. This loose fraternal organization also initiated a popular-style theological pamphlet series entitled *Concern,* a series "for questions of Christian renewal." Amid this ferment, Yoder took aim at his mentor, both personally and as a symbol of North American Mennonites. In a short article with a long title, "Reflections on the Irrelevance of Certain Slogans to the Historical Movements They Represent, Or, the Cooking of the Anabaptist Goods, Or, Ye Garnish the Sepulchres of the Righteous," Yoder openly challenged Bender's attempt to make Mennonites into just another form of Protestantism, just another of the denominations proliferating in North America. One can sense rather poignantly the growing pains Yoder was experiencing when he writes:

What has happened to me is that in the process of growing up, I have put together an interest in Anabaptism, which you gave me, an MCC experience to which you were instrumental in assigning me, and theological study to which you directed me, to come out with what is a more logical fruition of your own convictions than you yourself realize.[6]

Whatever one makes of the comparison with Bender here, it is important to note that, as this volume demonstrates, Yoder frequently returns to the importance of a broad, ecumenical view of Christianity that challenges the narrowness of both Mennonite and Protestant denominationalism.

When Yoder finally returned to the United States in 1957, he did not assume an academic position. Instead, he spent his first year working at J. S. Yoder and Son greenhouses in Wooster, Ohio. But this was not to be his long-term vocation. In 1959, Yoder began a job as an administrative assistant for the Mennonite Board of Missions, a job he held until 1965. Further reinforcing the ecumenical sensibilities developed in Europe, he came into contact with a broad range of Christians through the National Association of Evangelicals, the National Council of Churches, and the World Council of Churches during this time.

The inevitable pull of the academy, however, reappeared in the midst of this work. The transition began with teaching occasional courses back at Goshen College, and Yoder eventually found himself teaching full time, in 1965, at Goshen Biblical Seminary (where he subsequently also served as president and acting dean). Just two short years after beginning to teach full time, Yoder also started to explore the opportunity to teach occasionally at the University of Notre Dame, Catholic university just thirty miles to the northwest. Ten year later, in 1977, Yoder joined the Notre Dame faculty full time (with Goshen buying a small portion of his time). One can only speculate as to why Yoder left Goshen for Notre Dame. One thing, however, is clear: Yoder had already received a significant amount of theological notoriety through the publication of *The Politics of Jesus* (1972) years before leaving both the comforts and the distresses of his familiar Mennonite institutional home.

Yoder's tenure at Notre Dame overlapped with several prominent theological voices — Stanley Hauerwas and David Burrell among others — and even though it might have seemed like an odd place for a Mennonite theologian and ethicist, Notre Dame provided a rich intellectual environment that would have been somewhat comparable to his earlier years in Basel. At Notre Dame Yoder also found colleagues with a common vision. For example, in the late 1960s, after the series of assassinations that rocked the United States, several faculty members from Notre Dame, including Yoder, began conversations to explore the possible ways in which higher education could create a national climate in which violence could be lessened. These conversations served as the foundation of what would become the Kroc Institute for International Peace Studies at Notre Dame, of which Yoder was a fellow at the time of his death.

Just because Yoder became a professor and settled down (more or less) to teaching and writing does not mean he stopped traveling. In 1966, he traveled to South America, where he delivered a series of lectures; in 1970, he returned to Buenos Aires for a year, during which he really began to grasp the deep similarities between liberation theology, Judaism, and his own Mennonite position. As with his experience in France, somehow Yoder listened his way into the context and dialogues in South America to the extent that he was later made an honorary member of the Latin American Theological Fraternity. Further, he spent a year at the Tantur Ecumenical Institute for Advanced Theological Studies in Israel (1975–1976) where he deepened his understanding of Judaism and its complex relation to Christianity. The list of his travels could go on, but it need not. In all, Yoder lectured in over twenty countries in Latin America, Asia, and western Europe, as well as in South Africa, Poland, and Australia.

During these later years at Notre Dame, Yoder's intellectual reputation grew through the publication of new texts, the republication of older material, and not least through the efforts of his former Notre Dame colleague Stanley Hauerwas (now at Duke University) to make his work available and understood.

Before turning to a brief survey of Yoder's thought, however, a few final comments are in order.

It should be clear, by this point, that Yoder was a tireless worker. Unfortunately, this work was often performed at the expense of his family. In correspondence, his colleague William Klassen once directly challenged Yoder, admonishing him for his neglect of his family. Yoder responded rather characteristically, "What you say is obviously true about children's needs." Yet, he continued, "I'm theologically unable to justify a preoccupation with one's own family over against other needs and other people's worse-off children; but in my present running I'm not doing the others much good either."[7] This is but one example that there was indeed failure in Yoder's personal life. And there were others. For example, from the summer of 1992 to the summer of 1996, Yoder submitted to a long and difficult church disciplinary process for the purpose of addressing his role in inappropriate and damaging extramarital relations. Yet even in these difficult times, the importance of the integrity of the community of believers trumped other considerations as he was eventually restored to full communion.

The last years of Yoder's life were further complicated by a car accident that left him uncomfortably hobbling on crutches and almost constantly in pain. Yet in the midst of all this, Yoder continued working. On December 30, 1997 — the day after he celebrated his seventieth birthday with his extended family — Yoder was back at work, as usual, by six in the morning. Sometime late that morning, he collapsed outside of his office on the third floor of Decio Hall at Notre Dame and died of an aortic aneurysm. There are many ways to bring a short account of Yoder's life to an end, but perhaps the most appropriate one is that offered by Tom Yoder Neufeld, his son-in-law. In his eulogy, Tom noted that Yoder was a treasure in an earthen vessel. But clay jars are cracked and often leak and, even at the best of times, they have rough and chipped edges. At the worst of times they fall and break, and then the sharp edges of the shards can cut and wound, and wound deeply.[8] So, for all his intellectual gifts, Yoder was a humbled man, a frail man, a rather ordinary man. Yet his vision, communicated through his writings and his speaking, is extraordinary and contagious. To this we now turn.

An Extraordinary Vision

Many of Yoder's readers have entered his corpus through *The Politics of Jesus,* the groundbreaking text that brought together his Anabaptist pacifist convictions with much of what he had learned about Biblical Realism while in Basel. Against the background of the interminable hostilities in Vietnam, Yoder provided a coherent and compelling account of a political Jesus, a Jesus actually tempted by the Zealot option yet also a Messiah whose very suffering and death on the cross constituted a political act in solidarity with the poor and oppressed of this world, a Jesus whose kingdom was not some transcendent reality beyond this life, a Jesus who demanded imitation in the form of replacing dominion with servanthood and hostility with forgiveness.[9]

Certainly, these familiar themes from *The Politics of Jesus* are central to Yoder's thought. Yet they are also contextualized by texts that appeared as many as twenty years earlier and twenty-five years later (not to mention the posthumously published writings). In this wide array of writings, the vision that emerges is neither a vision of stark moral obedience to Jesus' commands nor a vision of strict literal interpretation of the Bible. Rather, it is a vision of God's rule and the church's participation in it, both in this world and the one to come. It is a communal vision, rooted in the life and teachings of Jesus and empowered by the Holy Spirit, that encompasses the entirety of humanity. To prescind from these summary statements for a moment, however, please allow a few comments concerning several constituent elements of Yoder's vision.

First, it must be noted that although Yoder is best known for his theological ethics, he did not consider himself an expert in this field (or the individual fields of theology or ethics, for that matter). He entered discourses in history, biblical studies, theology, ethics, peace studies, and, in his later years, sociology as well, moving easily and fluidly through the carefully cordoned boundaries of academic expertise. He called himself a dilettante, respectfully (and sometimes not so respectfully) challenging experts in their own fields. This he accomplished most often not by offering new answers to old questions but by asking new questions.

Second, although there is an overall coherence to his thought, Yoder's spiritual vision is never articulated in a systematic manner. He was a prolific memo writer; he liked to make and tediously revise lists; some might even say that he was a "revolutionary pamphleteer."[10] And, it is worth noting that the individual pieces that collectively constitute Yoder's corpus are frequently occasional or invited writings that were prepared for a particular audience with a particular agenda. For Yoder, this is entirely normal as his theology, like his account of the church, is situated within the contingencies of history.

Third, for the Christian, the vision begins with the life and teaching of Jesus, the particular revelation of how God works. For Yoder, one is not asked to believe in Jesus but to follow and participate in the life of Jesus (as if, in some way, belief could be separated from following). In this way, Christ's obedience to God expresses the way in which Christians too ought to follow God. Because Christ died on the cross, patiently allowing others to choose evil over obedience, so too Christians are called to follow Christ in nonviolence. He bravely writes, "The cross of Jesus is the extreme demonstration that *agape* seeks neither effectiveness nor justice, and is willing to suffer any loss or seeming defeat for the sake of obedience."[11] In short, Christians are to live and love like Jesus, know that in spite of the way things appear, God's purposes will prevail with the coming of God's kingdom: the resurrection of Jesus is proof that love cannot be conquered even if evil does its worst. With this assurance, Christians do not need to seek to control, to make things come out right. This is the note that Yoder continually sounded against Reinhold Niebuhr's form of Christian Realism, which dominated so much of Protestant ethics in the middle of the twentieth century. Writing in *The Politics of Jesus,* this note resounds loud and clear:

> The key to the obedience of God's people is not their effectiveness but their patience. The triumph of the right is assured not by the might that comes to the aid of the right, which is of course the justification of the use of violence and other kinds of power in every human conflict. The triumph of the right, although it is assured, is sure because of the power of the resurrection and not because of any calculation of causes and effects, nor because of the inherently greater strength of the good guys. The relationship between the obedience of God's people and the triumph of God's cause is not a relationship of cause and effect but one of cross and resurrection.[12]

Fourth and building on the previous, Yoder's vision cannot be instantiated individually, which is to say that following God is a communal activity. Although this theme is incipient in his early writings, the public role of the worshiping community emerges with considerable clarity as the corpus develops. Perhaps the most robust statement in this direction is his claim that worship "is the communal cultivation of an alternative construction of society and history."[13] The sacraments, therefore, are the embodied behaviors that constitute the church; they are the mode of participating in God's reconciling work in the world. Resisting the Protestant tendency to elevate the spoken word, Yoder argues that these behaviors or practices — forgiveness, baptism, the breaking of bread, and binding and loosing, to name a few — are the proclamation of the gospel. He explains as follows:

> When the family head feeds you at his or her table, the bread for which he or she has given thanks, you are part of the family. The act does not merely *mean* that you are part of the family. To take the floor in a community dialogue does not mean that you are part of the group; it *is* operational group membership. To be immersed and to

rise from the waters of the *mikvah* may be said to symbolize death and resurrection, but really it makes you a
member of the historical community of the new age.[14]

Through time, we are literally participants, through the work
of the Holy Spirit, in God's persistent and endlessly ingenious
offering of new creation and reconciliation. This is life in the
body of Christ.

Of course, this view of the sacraments offends many high-
church Christians and, given Yoder's context at Notre Dame,
it wouldn't be the first time he faced this objection. Yet he
persisted in calling the church to faithfully practice these sacraments, these instruments of social process, because he believed
that only in sharing these practices would the church become
truly united, both within itself and with God in Christ.

Fifth, having noted Yoder's emphasis on not seeking to make
things turn out right, it is now time to note a movement in
his thought that runs beneath and contextualizes this emphasis. Yoder's conviction that God will triumph and his concern
for the faithful practices of the church are rooted in a vision of
reality in which God's way of loving nonviolently aligns with
the inner logic of the created world and human existence as
God intended it to be. These practices follow "the grain of
the universe" in the same way Jesus did. On this foundation,
Yoder's cosmic vision embraces the goal of all humanity, becoming the community that the church is already called to be, the
goal that Yoder sees becoming realized in many corners of the
world, from Russia (Tolstoy) to India (Gandhi) to Latin America (Esquivel and Câmara). Yes, the church already knows what
the world does not yet know, but both are called to live in
right relationship with each other and with God as God loves
and rules both. It is the church's role to display an existence
that aligns with the grain of the universe, a public and political display that the rest of the world can see and embrace. And,
because of this, Yoder's vision is, as the title of the last book he
published before he died, for the nations.[15]

About This Volume

Yoder often bristled at the language of "spirituality." He energetically resisted separating the spiritual from the physical or describing spirituality as an expression of piety, as inwardness, or as mystical in any way. Yet he did not reject the language of spirituality entirely. For Yoder, spirituality is public, political, and part of everyday existence. As the epigraph for this volume, we have selected a passage from Yoder's posthumously published *Nonviolence: A Brief History* that aptly indicates Yoder's version of spirituality:

> Before it is a social strategy, nonviolence is a moral commitment; before it is a moral commitment, it is a distinctive spirituality. It presupposes and fosters a distinct way of seeing oneself and one's neighbor under God. That "way of seeing" is more like prayer than it is like a shrewd social strategy, although it is both. It is more a faith than a theory, although it is both.[16]

It is our hope that the pages of this volume expound and illuminate the manifold refractions that are intimated in this succinct definition.

To aid in this exploration, we have ordered the readings thematically, loosely following the logic outlined in the previous section, beginning with the meaning of Jesus, moving through the mandate of the church, and leading to his cosmic vision. To conclude the volume, we offer samples of how Yoder addressed practical and day-to-day considerations in light of the breadth of his vision. Further, each individual section begins with a prefatory guide to indicate the logic of the placement of the selections within it.

A final note: because Yoder published in many different contexts over many years, we have taken the liberty of (a) introducing occasional alterations in capitalization, spelling, and punctuation to maintain consistency and (b) normalizing gender-inclusive language (as Yoder himself was doing in his later publications).

NOTES

1. See Mark Nation, *John Howard Yoder: Mennonite Patience, Evangelical Witness, Catholic Convictions* (Grand Rapids, Mich.: Eerdmans, 2006), 3. This is an excellent introduction to Yoder's biography. For a more detailed account of Yoder's early years, see also Earl Zimmerman, *Practicing the Politics of Jesus: The Origin and Significance of John Howard Yoder's Social Ethics* (Telford, Pa.: Cascadia, 2007).

2. Nation, *John Howard Yoder,* 9.

3. See Harold S. Bender, *The Anabaptist Vision* (Scottsdale, Pa.: Herald Press, 1944).

4. Albert Keim, *Harold S. Bender, 1897–1962* (Scottsdale, Pa.: Herald Press, 1998), 460.

5. Ibid.

6. Ibid., 453.

7. See William Klassen, "John Howard Yoder and the Ecumenical Church," *Conrad Grebel Review* 16 (Spring): 80.

8. See "Tributes to John Howard Yoder (1927–1997): Given at His Memorial Service, January 2, 1998, at Goshen College Mennonite Church, Ind.," *Conrad Grebel Review* 16 (Spring): 95.

9. See Yoder, *The Politics of Jesus: Vicit Agnus Noster,* 2nd ed. (Grand Rapids, Mich.: Eerdmans, 1994), 131.

10. See the introduction to John Howard Yoder, *Preface to Theology: Christology and Theological Method,* ed. Stanley Hauerwas and Alex Sider (Grand Rapids, Mich.: Brazos Press, 2002), 9.

11. John Howard Yoder, *Christian Attitudes to War, Peace, and Reconciliation,* ed. Theodore J. Koontz and Andy Alexis-Baker (Grand Rapids, Mich.: Brazos Press, 2009), 319.

12. Yoder, *The Politics of Jesus,* 232.

13. John Howard Yoder, *The Priestly Kingdom: Social Ethics as Gospel* (Notre Dame, Ind.: University of Notre Dame Press, 1984), 43.

14. John Howard Yoder, *The Royal Priesthood: Essays Eschatological and Ecumenical,* ed. Michael G. Cartwright (Scottdale, Pa.: Herald Press, 1998), 366.

15. See John Howard Yoder, *For Nations: Essays Public and Evangelical* (Grand Rapids, Mich.: Eerdmans, 1997).

16. John Howard Yoder, *Nonviolence: A Brief History — The Warsaw Lectures,* ed. Paul Martens, Matthew Porter, and Myles Werntz (Waco, Tex.: Baylor University Press, 2010), 43.

1

The Meaning of Jesus

God chose to be revealed through the particular, through the particular works and words of a particular man, Jesus Christ. This is the beginning of Yoder's theology and everything else finds its place in relation to this fundamental conviction. For this reason, the meaning of Jesus must be the theme for the first series of readings in this volume.

The first reading included here serves as a preliminary introduction to the three roles of Jesus in Yoder's thought. Reflecting his concern for unity in words and works, Jesus is portrayed in the familiar roles of teacher and model. Within and above these two roles stands a third: Jesus as a public figure, a political figure. The public and political nature of Jesus' life and teaching inflects all that Yoder has to say about Jesus and, therefore, all that Yoder has to say about anything else.

The remaining readings in this series have been selected to illuminate the many ways in which the public and political nature of Jesus shape Yoder's construal of the life and teaching of Jesus. They begin with a few comments concerning Jesus' Jewish background and move through his proclamation of a new age to his death on a cross, which, in turn, defines the entirety of Christian existence. The bulk of the subsequent selections reveal that Yoder is wrestling with and against traditional appropriations of the cross of Christ in an attempt to provide a more adequate account of Christian existence as suffering love, as communal resistance to the temptations of violence and power, as participation in the patient nonviolent work of God.

After establishing the centrality of the person of Jesus in Yoder's thought, the final three readings briefly outline his articulation of the way in which the early church read the life and teachings of Jesus within the larger context of scripture and history. In this way, the first series provides the foundation for understanding the importance of the church — the body of Christ — which is the theme of the second series of readings.

WHO IS JESUS?

Jesus as Public Figure

The first thing to say about the biblical picture is that Jesus is a public figure. He uses political language. The authorities perceive him as a political threat and put him to death because of it. We can discuss what share the Jews and Romans had in his death. But it is clear, hypocritically or honestly, that the legal basis for his crucifixion in the Roman record books was the charge that he was an insurrectionist. That charge is the reason for an inscription on the cross, reported in all four gospels. He was accused of being the king of the Jews. We may still debate whether there was falseness in the accusation or in other details about the process, but that accusation was the formal ground for his execution.

Jesus as Teacher

What ideas help make sense of Jesus' new stance in society? This new way of being political, through being the "other" community, embodies alternative political options and expresses and implies new ideas. Here we will not spend time, useful as that would be, digging through all the teachings of Jesus. But one element is certainly the proclamation of the kingdom as a

new age in world history. The kingdom is at hand. The Beatitudes say, "The kingdom is at hand, so *good for you* !" They are
not simply a series of virtue statements; they do not say, "You
ought to be a peacemaker, because God likes peacemakers."
Instead they say, "The kingdom is here: blessed are the poor,
because in the kingdom the poor are the people who are at
home." Certainly one assumption of the ethic of Jesus is that
the new age has come; it is at hand.

Another characteristic of Jesus' ethic is a strengthened sense
of the presence of the Father in our life. God is described as
father, not simply as judge or providential sovereign. God is a
loving, suffering father who loves the evil people as much as
he loves the good. Jesus often tells us to be like himself. But
Matthew 5 is the only place where Jesus says we will be like the
Father — when we love our enemies.

Another obvious theme in Matthew 5 and 6 is the fulfillment
of the law. The law is not set aside. It is rounded out, intensified.

Jesus as Model

So we have Jesus as public figure and Jesus as teacher. But Jesus
is also pattern. We do not have one frozen model for thinking
about the life of the believer in relationship to Jesus. This fundamental stance works itself out in many different styles. Jesus
is our model in many ways having to do with death and suffering. That suffering is not for its own sake but is the cost of
the kind of involvement in the world that he represented and to
which he calls us.

Jesus is not generally a model in the New Testament. He was
celibate, as far as we can tell, but even when the apostle Paul is
arguing that it is good to remain unmarried, he does not appeal
to the model of Jesus. Jesus worked with his hands as some
kind of builder for a while, yet when Paul extols the virtue of
working with one's hands as a tentmaker, he does not appeal
to the example of Jesus. So Jesus is appealed to as an example
not generally but only at the point of the meaning of the cross.

On *that* subject he is *always* appealed to. Every major strand of
New Testament literature has this thought in its foundation.
— *Christian Attitudes to War, Peace,*
and Revolution, 314–15

WHY THE JEWISHNESS
OF JESUS MATTERS

The readiness to be atypical, to be nonconformed, of which I
have just been writing, is strengthened by one further turn of the
argument in which Jewish thought had already taken the path
that Jesus followed further, and that later rabbis took still further. This is the preference for the concrete case. *Halakah,* the
tradition about specific behavior, is clarified and codified sooner
and more firmly than *aggadah,* the vision of things in a world
under God that make such behavior reasonable. The concrete
shape of the culture of faithfulness is more crucial to a people's
commonality of commitment than is the piety with which it is
filled out, kept alive, personalized, and explained to outsiders.

Imperatives like "go the second mile" or "first be reconciled
with your brother" or "swear not at all," or reality readings like
"whoever marries a divorced woman commits adultery" or "if
you do not forgive others God will not forgive you" are more
transculturally translatable, and more foundational in defining
a community's identity, than the more abstract "first principles"
from which academics would like to say they are "derived."
We moderns would like first to say something formal like "so
act that your behavior could be a rule for everyone." Then we
would like to say something substantial but broad like "the
nature of marriage is . . ." or "every person has a right to. . . ."
Only a few logical steps later would we then be willing to get
down to specific duties and decisions.

Jesus, Jewry, and the minority churches do it the other way.
They first name representative acts that are imperative or excluded. This is *halakah.* Then *aggadah,* "spirituality," considers
why such judgments make good sense.

The tilt toward concreteness can be overdone, of course. It has shortcomings in the face of rapid cultural change or in the face of ecumenical challenge. It can become "legalism" in the bad sense of that term. It can build a barrier in the way of cross-cultural communication or service. Here, however, we are discussing what originally made a commitment to love the enemy and to renounce violence credible and viable in its challenge to the ethos of establishment.

It was the Jewishness of Jesus, the rootage of his message in the particular heritage of Abraham, Moses, and Jeremiah, that, as we have seen, made it good news for the whole world. There were other peace philosophers and peace prophets in the Ancient Near East. Only the Jewish world vision, effective in Jochanan and the entire stream of non-Zealot rabbinism, which he catalyzed, could make of accepting powerlessness not only a viable compromise but an identity, to make Jewry, beyond the collapse of the Jerusalem polity, into a new kind of culture viable without a state. Only the Jew Jesus, by announcing and accomplishing the fulfillment of God's promises to the Jews, could send out into the world a people of peace open to the Gentiles. Only the Jewish claim that the one true God, known to Abraham's children through their history, was also the Creator and sustainer of the other peoples as well, could enable mission without provincialism, cosmopolitan vision without empire.... — *The Jewish-Christian Schism Revisited,* 74–75

THE NEW AGE OF JESUS

We cannot assume that we know exactly what was meant by Jesus' statement that "this word is fulfilled." In what sense was Jesus claiming that something was beginning to happen right then in his person? Did anything really happen at all? Was he announcing an event the realization of which was dependent on the faith of his listeners, so that it could not come to pass after all because of their unbelief? Or was he announcing what actually then did happen, namely, nothing very visible for a while?

This is a serious question. But let us recognize that it is a question of systematic hermeneutics read into the Lucan text by readers who were not there. It has to do with the sense in which the fulfillment Jesus promised was a historical reality. It does not, however, have anything to do with the clear affirmation that the subject of the text is a social event. We may have great difficulty in knowing in what sense this event came to pass or could have come to pass; but what the event was supposed to be is clear: it is a visible sociopolitical, economic restructuring of relations among the people of God, achieved by divine intervention in the person of Jesus as the one Anointed and endued with the Spirit.

The second theme of the encounter in the synagogue provides Jesus' first direct offense to his hearers; appealing to prophetic precedent, he proclaims the opening of the New Age to Gentiles. This second thrust does not seem to be derived from the jubilee proclamation; it grows rather out of Jesus' response to the disbelief bred in his hearers by their familiarity with his family. There is rather a negative correlation between the two themes; the undercutting of racial egoism by the second thrust prevented the former from being taken in a nationalistic sense. The prophet's reference to the captive and oppressed can thus not refer to Israel or Judaism at large as collectively oppressed; the liberation is too wide for that. The New Age is for all, and the hesitance of the Nazarenes to believe will only hasten its wider proclamation....

After the move to Capernaum (Luke 4:31) Luke reports a rising tide of effectiveness among the multitudes, the sick, and the tax-gatherers. Soon the backlash of the religious establishment begins, with objections to Jesus' authority to forgive (5:21) and his disreputable associates (5:30). Almost immediately the opposition mounts to the point of angry scheming (6:11). Luke emphasizes that it was "in these days" that Jesus, after a night-long vigil, named twelve key messengers, firstfruits of a restored Israel. To organized opposition he responds with the formal founding of a new social reality. New teachings are no threat, as long as the teacher stands alone; a movement, extending his personality in both time and space, presenting an alternative to the structures that were there before, challenges the system as no mere words ever could.

Cognate as the *functioning* of this inner circle may have been to the way any other rabbi would live with his favored disciples, there is more to its *formation* than that. Their number, the night of prayer, and the following ceremonial proclamation of woes and blessings all serve to dramatize a new stage of publicness. The opening beyond Judaism which was predicted in the synagogue at Nazareth is now beginning; the "seacoast of Tyre and Sidon" is represented on this great plain. Despite the extensive parallels with the Sermon on the Mount, the emphasis in Luke's report is different. The blessings are balanced with woes, after the fashion of ancient Israel's covenant ceremonies. The blessing is for the poor, not only the poor in spirit; for the hungry, not only those who hunger for justice. The examples drawn from the sexual realm (Matt. 5:27–32) are missing; only personal and economic conflict are chosen as specimens of the New Way, in which seized property is not reclaimed and the delinquent loan is forgiven. As in the jubilee, and as in the Lord's Prayer, *debt* is seen as the paradigmatic social evil. In short, the announcement of the synagogue is being repeated and spelled out in detail, this time with a structured social base (both the believing multitude and the defined nucleus) and in plain view of the crowds ("in the hearing of the people" [7:1]). An ethic to be guided by the twin loci of imitating the boundless love of God for his rebellious children (6:35–36) and being strikingly different from the ordinary "natural law" behavior of others ("What credit is that to you? Even sinners . . . " [6:32–34]) is conceivable only if a new age has begun, and if that age's novelty is at the point of economic realism. . . .

The brief warning "not peace but a sword" is immediately expanded into an extended passage (14:25ff). It is just when "great multitudes were accompanying him" that Jesus speaks his first severe public word of warning:

If anyone does not hate father and mother and wife and
children and brothers and sisters, yea and even his own
life, he cannot be my disciple.

Modern psychologizing interpretation of Jesus has been
bothered largely with whether the word "hate" here should
be taken seriously or not. This is certainly to miss the point of
the passage. The point is rather that in a society characterized
by very stable, religiously undergirded family ties, Jesus is here
calling into being a community of voluntary commitment, willing for the sake of its calling to take upon itself the hostility of
the given society....

There are thus about the community of disciples those sociological traits most characteristic of those who set about to
change society: a visible structured fellowship, a sober decision
guaranteeing that the costs of commitment to the fellowship
have been consciously accepted, and a clearly defined lifestyle is
different, not because of arbitrary rules separating the believer's
behavior from that of "normal people," but because of the
exceptionally normal quality of humanness to which the community is committed. The distinctness is not a cultic or ritual
separation, but rather a nonconformed quality of ("secular")
involvement in the life of the world. It thereby constitutes an
unavoidable challenge to the powers that be and the beginning
of a new set of social alternatives....

Jesus was not just a moralist whose teachings had some
political implications; he was not primarily a teacher of spirituality whose public ministry unfortunately was seen in a
political light; he was not just a sacrificial lamb preparing for
his immolation, or a God-Man whose divine status calls us
to disregard his humanity. Jesus was, in his divinely mandated
(i.e., promised, anointed, messianic) prophethood, priesthood,
and kingship, the bearer of a new possibility of human, social,
and therefore political relationships. His baptism is the inaugu-
ration and his cross is the culmination of that new regime in
which his disciples are called to share. Hearers or readers may
choose to consider that kingdom as not real, or not relevant, or

not possible, or not inviting; but no longer can we come to this choice in the name of systematic theology or honest hermeneutics. At this one point there is no difference between the Jesus of *Historie* and the Christ of *Geschichte,* or between Christ as God and Jesus as human, or between the religion of Jesus and the religion about Jesus (or between the Jesus of the canon and the Jesus of history). No such slicing can avoid his call to an ethic marked by the cross, a cross identified as the punishment of a person who threatens society by creating a new kind of community leading a radically new kind of life.

— *The Politics of Jesus,* 32–34, 37, 39, 52–53

THE CROSS OF CHRIST

The believer's cross is no longer any and every kind of suffering, sickness, or tension, the bearing of which is demanded. The believer's cross is, like that of Jesus, the price of social nonconformity. It is not, like sickness or catastrophe, an inexplicable, unpredictable suffering; it is the end of a path freely chosen after counting the cost. It is not, like Luther's or Thomas Müntzer's or Zinzendorf's or Kierkegaard's cross or *Anfechtung,* an inward wrestling of the sensitive soul with self and sin; it is the social reality of representing in an unwilling world the Order to come. The Word: "The servant is not greater than his master. If they persecuted me they will persecute you" (John 15:20) is not a pastoral counsel to help with the ambiguities of life; it is a normative statement about the relation of our social obedience to the messianity of Jesus. Representing as he did the divine order now at hand, accessible; renouncing as he did the legitimate use of violence and the accrediting of the existing authorities; renouncing as well the ritual purity of noninvolvement, his people will encounter in ways analogous to his own the hostility of the old order.

Being human, Jesus must have been subject somehow or other to the testings of pride, envy, anger, sloth, avarice, gluttony, and lust, but it does not enter into the concerns of the gospel writer to give us any information about any struggles he may have had with their attraction. The one temptation the human Jesus faced — and faced again and again — as a constitutive element of his public ministry, was the temptation to exercise social responsibility, in the interest of justified revolution, through the use of available violent methods. Social withdrawal was no temptation to him; that option (which most Christians take part of the time) was excluded at the outset. Any alliance with the Sadducean establishment in the exercise of conservative social responsibility (which most Christians choose the rest of the time) was likewise excluded at the outset. We understand Jesus only if we can empathize with this threefold rejection: the self-evident, axiomatic, sweeping rejection of both quietism and establishment responsibility, and the difficult, constantly reopened, genuinely attractive option of the crusade.

The statement of the problem with which we began was drawn not from Luke but from the present. Because Jesus is not meant to be taken as normative for political ethics, it is said, we must obviously, consciously, properly get our ethics elsewhere, from a "responsible" calculation of our chances and our duty to make events come out as well as possible. This substitution of nature or history for Jesus as the locus of revelation was justified by the claim that Jesus had nothing to say on this subject. But now we see that he did have something to say; in fact that he said little that was not somehow on this subject. The gospel record refuses to let the modern social ethicist off the hook. It is quite possible to refuse to accept Jesus as normative, but it is not possible on the basis of the record to declare him irrelevant....

His disavowal of Peter's well-intentioned effort to defend him cannot be taken out of the realm of ethics by the explanation that he had to get himself immolated in order to satisfy the requirements of some metaphysically motivated doctrine of the atonement; it was because God's will for God's servant in this world is that he should renounce legitimate defense. When Jesus wrestled repeatedly with the tempter, from the desert at the beginning to the garden at the end, this was not a clumsily contrived morality play meaning to teach us that kingship was no temptation; it was because God's servant in this world was facing and rejecting the claim that the exercise of social responsibility through the use of self-evidently necessary means is a moral duty....

As long as readers could stay unaware of the political/social dimension of Jesus' ministry (which most of Christendom seems to have done quite successfully), then it was also possible to perceive the "in Christ" language of the epistles as mystical or the "dying with Christ" as psychologically morbid. But if we may posit — as after the preceding pages we must — that the asspostles had and taught at least a core memory of their Lord's earthly ministry in its blunt historicity, then this centering of the apostolic ethic upon the disciple's cross evidences a substantial, binding, and sometimes costly social stance. There have perhaps been times when the issues of power, violence, and peoplehood were not at the center of ethical preoccupations; but in the waning twentieth century they certainly are. The rediscovery of this ethic of "responsibility" or of "power" can no longer at the same time claim to be Christian and bypass the judgment of the promise of the Suffering Servant's exemplarity....

One universal demand that the church as an agency of counsel and consolation must meet is the need of men and women of all ages for help in facing suffering: illness and accidents, loneliness and defeat. What more fitting resource could there be than the biblical language that makes suffering bearable, meaningful within God's purposes, even meritorious in that "bearing one's cross" is a synonym for discipleship? Hosts of sincere people in hospitals or in conflict-ridden situations have been helped by this thought to bear the strain of their destiny with a sense of divine presence and purpose.

Yet our respect for the quality of these lives and the validity of this pastoral concern must not blind us to the abuse of language and misuse of scripture they entail. The cross of Christ was not an inexplicable or chance event that happened to strike him, like illness or accident. To accept the cross as his destiny, to move toward it and even to provoke it, when he could well have done otherwise, was Jesus' constantly reiterated free choice. He warns his disciples lest their embarking on the same path be less conscious of its costs (Luke 14:25–33). The cross of Calvary was not a difficult family situation, not a frustration of visions of personal fulfillment, a crushing debt, or a nagging in-law; it was the political, legally-to-be-expected result of a moral clash with the powers ruling his society. Already the early Christians had to be warned against claiming merit for any and all suffering; only if their suffering is innocent, and a result of the evil will of their adversaries, may it be understood as meaningful before God (1 Pet. 2:18–21; 3:14–18; 4:1, 13–16; 5:9; James 4:10).

Another transposition makes the cross an inward experience of the self. This is found in Thomas Müntzer, in Zinzendorf, in revivalism, and in Christian existentialism....

The other direction in which "cross" language can evolve is that of subjective brokenness, the renunciation of pride and self-will. Bonhoeffer's *Life Together* speaks of "breaking through to the cross" as occurring in confession. "In confession we affirm and accept our cross." Our sharing in Christ's death, he continues, is the "shameful death of the sinner in confession." A similar thrust is typical of the Keswick family of renewal movements in Anglo-Saxon Protestantism. We may agree that the humility of confession may be quite desirable for mental health, for group processes, and for the creation of community, but this should not keep us from realizing that "cross" is not the word for that in the New Testament.

— *The Politics of Jesus*, 96–97, 98, 127–30

Jesus' interest was in humanity; the reason for his low esteem for the political order was his high, loving esteem for humans as the concrete objects of his concern. Christ is *agape*; self-giving, nonresistant love. At the cross this nonresistance, including the refusal to use political means of self-defense, found its ultimate revelation in the uncomplaining and forgiving death of the innocent at the hands of the guilty. This death reveals how God deals with evil; here is the only valid starting point for

Christian pacifism or nonresistance. The cross is the extreme demonstration that *agape* seeks neither effectiveness nor justice and is willing to suffer any loss or seeming defeat for the sake of obedience.

But the cross is not defeat. Christ's obedience unto death was crowned by the miracle of the resurrection and the exaltation at the right hand of God.

> Bearing the human likeness, revealed in human shape, he humbled himself, and in obedience accepted even death — death on a cross. Therefore God raised him to the heights and bestowed on him the name above all names. (Phil. 2:8–10)

Effectiveness and success had been sacrificed for the sake of love, but this sacrifice was turned by God into a victory that vindicated to the utmost the apparent impotence of love. The same life of the new aeon revealed in Christ is also the possession of the church, since Pentecost answered the Old Testament's longings for a "pouring out of the Spirit on all flesh" and a "law written in the heart." The Holy Spirit is the "down payment" on the coming glory, and the new life of the resurrection is the path of the Christian now. But before the resurrection there was the cross, and Christians must follow their Master in suffering for the sake of love.

Nonresistance is thus not a matter of legalism but of discipleship, not "thou shalt not" but "as he is so are we in this world" (1 John 4:17), and it is especially in relation to evil that discipleship is meaningful. Every strand of New Testament literature testifies to a direct relationship between the way Christ suffered on the cross and the way the Christian, as disciple, is called to suffer in the face of evil (Matt. 10:38; Mark 10:38–39; 8:34–35; Luke 14:27). Solidarity with Christ ("discipleship") must often be in tension with the wider human solidarity (John 15:20; 2 Cor. 1:5; 4:10; Phil. 1:29; 2:5–8; 3:10; Col. 1:24–25; Heb. 12:1–4; 1 Pet. 2:21–22; Rev. 12:11).

— *The Original Revolution*, 56–57

THE MEANING OF
THE RESURRECTION

The present meaning of resurrection for ethics is that we are never boxed in. As believers, we are not to be calculating on the basis of the assumption that we are boxed into a world in which there are no new options. Many "saving" events in history were unforeseeable, unplanned, but they happened. The resurrection was an impossible, unforeseeable new option, and it happened. We do not know what happened in such a way that we could take it to the American Medical Association and show them what shape the corpse is in now. We cannot show them how resurrection works with modern, scientific, causal models. Yet we are committed to confessing as relevant for our ethics that there is a power in history that reaches beyond the boxes in which we find ourselves. So one more reason that the cross is meaningful is that even though it fails, it does not fail if there is resurrection.

You cannot translate that reality into pagan social science until after it has happened. When you think you are in a blind alley, you do not know that the new thing can happen until it happens. Once the new thing happens, of course, then it was possible. Look at some of the most striking events that now matter for our history. They could not have happened. The Montgomery bus boycott should never have happened in terms of ordinary social process in the American South. Nothing about his biography should have created a Gandhi. Most important events in the forward movement of history could not have happened. You could not have predicted them by extrapolating from the year before. Yet they did happen. We have to figure them out after the fact. But if you had looked at the scene in terms of statistics and probability, lifestyles and educational models, most of these things would not have happened. So resurrection is a Christian model for reading world history. That's one more reason that we do not work on ordinary effectiveness and lesser-evil calculations.

— *Christian Attitudes to War, Peace,*
and Revolution, 319–20

JUSTIFICATION BY FAITH

Just as a guilty thief or murderer is still a thief or a murderer after a declaration of amnesty has freed him from his punishment, the argument runs, so a guilty sinner is still a sinner when God declares, on the ground of the work of Christ, which no person could have accomplished for himself or herself, that he or she shall henceforth be considered a new person, forgiven and restored to fellowship. But this "being considered" is, spiritually speaking, a legal fiction. It is valid only on the grounds of the sovereign authority of the judge who declared it to be so. The act of justification or the status of being just or righteous before God is therefore radically disconnected from any objective or empirical achievement of goodness by the believer.

This "disconnection" is only a part of the wider phenomenon of separation between body and soul, objective and subjective realities, outward and inward history, which are the key, are they not, to all the specific emphases of the apostle Paul?

Was not the central message of the apostle Paul his rejection of any objective dimension to the work of God that could be focused in piety, religious practices, or ethical behavior in such a way as to turn the believer's attention toward the human works instead of toward the gift of God? Does not the insistence that justification is by faith alone and through grace alone, apart from any correlation with works of any kind, undercut any radical and ethical concern by implication, even if Paul himself might not have been rigorous enough to push that implication all the way? If we truly join with classic Protestantism in considering the proclamation of justification by grace through faith to be the point at which the gospel stands or falls, must we not then interpret the ethical tradition that Paul took over from Jewish Christianity and shared with his Gentile churches as a vestige of another system, destined to fade away? Was it not, after all, at the cost of forgetting Paul's emphasis on grace that a later generation again made good works and a certain social stance very important in the preaching of the church? . . .

What then was Paul's understanding of sin? When he does speak of himself as a serious sinner at all, this is not because of his existential anguish under the righteousness of God in general, but very specifically because, not having recognized that Messiah had come in Jesus, he had persecuted the church and fought the opening of God's covenant to the Gentiles. What is now set right in his life is not that he has overcome his inner resistances and has become able to trust in God for his right status before God; it is rather that through the inexplicable intervention of God on the Damascus road and in later experiences, Paul has become the agent of the action of God for the right cause. He has become the privileged bearer of the cause of the ingathering of the Gentiles. . . .

The work of Christ is not only that he saves the souls of individuals and henceforth they can love each other better; the work of Christ, the making of peace, the breaking down of the wall, is itself the constituting of a new community made up of two kinds of people, those who had lived under the law and those who had not. The events the book of Acts narrates as the recent initiative of the Holy Spirit in opening up the churches, first in Jerusalem and then in Samaria, then in Damascus and Antioch, to the fellowship of believing Jews and believing Gentiles, are here interpreted by Paul, a major actor in that drama and its accredited interpreter, as being the extended meaning of the cross and resurrection of Jesus. . . .

But the proclamation that God reconciles classes of people is in itself far more than a double negative. To proclaim it as Paul did in his writings years and even decades after Pentecost is to confirm that such reconciliation is a real experience and therefore a real invitation. Paul is saying, somewhere toward the *end* of the evolution of apostolic Christianity, what Jesus had said somewhere near the beginning. That he can still say it now is proof that, at least to some modest degree, experience had confirmed it. Paul says that it characterizes the victory of God's creation-sustaining love that insider and outsider, friend and enemy are equally blessed, in such manner that the genuineness (Jesus said, "perfection") of our love is also made real at the point of its application to the enemy, the Gentile, the sinner. There is a sense in which the ethics of marriage and the prohibition of adultery, or the ethics of work and the regulation of attitudes toward slavery, or the opening up of communication and the prohibition of falsehood are all part of the promise of a new humanity enabled and created by God, and already being received by men and women of faith. But it is *par excellence* with reference to enmity between peoples, the extension of neighbor love to the enemy, and the renunciation of violence even in the most righteous cause, that this promise takes on flesh in the most original, the most authentic, the most frightening and scandalous, and therefore in the most evangelical way. It is the good news that my enemy and I are united, through no merit or work of our own, in a new humanity that forbids henceforth my ever taking his or her life in my hands.

— *The Politics of Jesus,* 213, 217, 219, 225–26

THE ROLE OF REPENTANCE

"The kingdom of God is at hand: repent and believe the good news!" To repent is not to feel bad but to think differently. Protestantism, and perhaps especially evangelical Protestantism, in its concern for helping all individuals to make their own authentic choice in full awareness and sincerity, is in constant danger of confusing the kingdom itself with the benefits of the kingdom. If any repent, if any turn around to follow Jesus in his new way of life, this will do something for the aimlessness of their life. It will do something for their loneliness by giving them fellowship. It will do something for their anxiety and guilt by giving them a good conscience. So the Bultmanns and the Grahams whose "evangelism" is to proclaim the offer of restored selfhood, liberation from anxiety and guilt, are not wrong. If any repent, it will do something for their intellectual confusion by giving them doctrinal meat to digest, a heritage to appreciate, and a conscience about telling it all as it is: So "evangelicalism" with its concern for hallowed truth and reasoned communication is not wrong; it is right. If one repents, it will do something for one's moral weakness by giving the focus for wholesome self-discipline; it will keep individuals from immorality and get people to work on time. So the Peales and Robertses who promise that God cares about helping me squeeze through the tight spots of life are not wrong; they have their place. BUT ALL OF THIS IS NOT THE GOSPEL. This is just the bonus, the wrapping paper thrown in when you buy the meat, the "everything" which will be added, without our taking thought for it, if we seek first the kingdom of God and his righteousness. . . .

Centuries of church history, both in the penitential principles of Catholic tradition and in the concern of Protestantism for personal integrity, have taught us to misunderstand radically what John the Baptist and Jesus meant when they began preaching, "Repent! For the kingdom is at hand!" Under "repentance" we think of remorse, regret, sorrow for sin. But what they were calling for was a transformation of the understanding (*metanoia*), a redirected will ready to live in a new kind of world.

The teachings that follow refuse to measure by the standards of "common sense" or "realism" or "reason"; they testify to the novelty of the kingdom that is at hand. Jesus will therefore be describing for us a morality of repentance or of conversion; not a prescription of what every person can and should do to be happy; not a meditation on how best to guide a society, but a description of how a person behaves whose life has been transformed by meeting Jesus.

—*The Original Revolution*, 31–32, 38

INDIVIDUALISM AND CONVERSION

If there is any one biblical text that focuses for lay understanding the individualism of the Pietist heritage it is the statement of 2 Corinthians 5:17: "If anyone be in Christ, *he is* a new creature." It has seemed self-evident that we were being promised here, overlapping with the language of a new birth (John 3:5–6), a metaphysical or ontological transformation of the individual person. The miracle of being made a new person has been promised in evangelistic proclamation and has served in turn to illuminate traditional understandings of the rootage of Christian social concern. It is because only a transformed individual will behave differently that some kinds of social activism are fruitless; it is because a transformed individual will definitely behave differently that the preaching of the gospel to individuals is the surest way to change society.

It is not the concern of the present study to deny that such a thrust has had a wholesome corrective impact in certain contexts in the history of Protestant thought and Protestant church life. Like Stendahl, we may concede a certain usefulness to nonbiblical thought patterns. Nor are we setting aside the "new birth" imagery of John 3 or parallel themes elsewhere. Our question is only whether this is what *Paul* is saying in *this* text. This becomes extremely doubtful when we look more carefully at the text itself.

As the italics in the Authorized Version indicate, the words "he is" are not in the original text. Now it can regularly be necessary to add the English "is" in order to make clear a predication, which in the Greek requires no copulative verb. But to add "he" (or "she"), thereby identifying an antecedent in the previous clause, is quite another matter. It is grammatically not impossible to reach back to the "anyone" earlier in the verse as the understood subject of this predication; but that is not the only interpretation, and others should be tried first.

A second shortcoming of this traditional interpretation of "the new creature" as the transformed individual personality is that the work *ktisis,* here translated "creature" or "creation," is not used elsewhere in the New Testament to designate the individual person. It in fact most often is used to designate not the object of creation but rather the act of creating (e.g., Rom. 1:20), "from the creation of the world." Secondarily, it may mean the entire universe (Mark 16:15; Col. 1:15, 24; Rom.

8:19–22; Heb. 9:11). The single reference to "human creation" refers to social institutions (1 Pet. 2:13). In the one other place where the phrase "new creation" is used, it is quite parallel to the "new humanity" of Ephesians 2:15, not a renewed individual but a new social reality, marked by the overcoming of the Jew/Greek barrier; "neither circumcision nor uncircumcision but a new creation" (Gal. 6:15).

Putting together these strictly linguistic observations, it becomes enormously more probable that we should lean to the kind of translation favored by more recent translators, literally, "if anyone is in Christ, new is creation," or more smoothly, "there is a whole new world" (NEB). The accent lies not on transforming the ontology of the person (to say nothing of transforming his or her psychological or neurological equipment) but on transforming the perspective of one who has accepted Christ as life context.

This is certainly the point of the rest of the passage in question. Paul is explaining why he no longer regards anyone from the human point of view, why he does not regard Jew as Jew or Greek as Greek, but rather looks at every person in the light of the new world that begins in Christ. "The old has passed away, behold the new has come," is a social or historical statement, not an introspective or emotional one.

— The Politics of Jesus, 221–23

What makes a person what he or she is in terms of what we usually call "personality" is profoundly correlated with the nervous system. Who a person is can be influenced by electric shocks applied to that nervous system, by chemicals, by brain surgery, and other kinds of intervention into the personality that are not mental or spiritual at all in the traditional understanding. Whatever the relationship of the life of the nervous system and the life of the spirit may be, at least there has to be some kind of serious correlation. For example, there is biochemical physiology, according to which a man or a woman is made into what he or she is by his or her DNA and continues to become and remains what he or she is by virtue of electrochemical events in nerve cells. These are the ways the first creation worked to make humanity human. Does the "new creation" work this way? Would sufficient sophistication enable us to find how conversion changes a person's DNA or his or her neural electrochemistry? If not, why not?

Another level of the reality of what it means to be a person is that which is dealt with by the various schools of psychology. There are behavior patterns that are learned and can be unlearned. There are complexes and syndromes that are the product of the interaction between the individual needs and appetites on one hand and the family and social environment on the other. Especially, certain major figures in the early life of a child and certain pivotal experiences in development through adolescence are generally understood to have much to do with defining who a person is. Does conversion change syndromes and complexes? If so, does it do so through experiences of learning and unlearning which are themselves subject to psychological interpretation? Or does it happen on some other level? Is the new birth a cathartic self-understanding? Does it provide one with a better father image (in God) or a better ego-model (in Jesus), which thereby enables one to cope more adequately?

There is also a pedagogical view of the nature of the whole person who is seen as learner, acquiring skills and awarenesses. Is conversion a "learning"? Does it fit on a scale of "moral development"?

These questions could be asked with an intention that might be flippant or destructive. That is not my intent. The fact needs simply to be faced that if we do claim in any concrete sense that the new birth changes who a person really is, we cannot avoid the encounter with questions of the kind that are asked by the secular disciplines, which also deal in their ways with what a person really is. Would we claim that conversion in the heart has no correlate in the biochemistry of the nerves or in the psychodynamics of the personality? Or do we argue a kind of correlation so that conversion could, with adequate tools, be measured by the psychologist or the neurologist?

I ask the question because it is impossible in our time to take the language of conversion seriously without asking it. But by asking it I have pointed out backhandedly that when the classic Protestant understanding of conversion developed in the first place, whether we think in the most precise sense of the most highly developed conversion theories of the revivalists of North America from Edwards to Finney, or whether we go back to the description of the faith that justifies (in Luther) or the vision of God (in the late medieval mystics), *none* of the people we would be trying to understand would have been saying *then* that conversion is an event in the field of psychodynamics or neurology. So whether we affirm some kind of positive correlation between several levels, or deny that there is any connection at all and thereby refuse to converse with the modern human sciences, in either case it raises questions of correlation that were not there before. The gospel promise of transformation talks about the human person as he or she really is; so do these other kinds of analyses. If they are all talking about the same person, then it would seem that we should expect that as they cover the same ground, their measurements and descriptions would somehow connect. Do we want our phrasing of the claims and promises of the gospel to be tested by these other disciplines? Or do we rather mean to take the other approach, that of compartmentalization, saying that though we all deal with the same human being, the ways we deal with him or her are not at all on the same level? There are several classical ways to try to resolve this problem, and all of them seem to have serious logical and practical shortcomings.

If a Christian really believes that there has been physical healing, such as the lengthening of a leg or the removal by miracle of a cancer, it will be a part of the authenticity of that witness to claim that X-rays or other medical verification could be appealed to. In a similar way, it probably should be assumed that if there is concrete reality to conversion as a change of what the person really is, it could be measured by the scientists. The fact that one does not see many conversionist Christians doing that scientific work does not necessarily prove they would not believe in it, nor that it could not be done. The fact that traditional conversionist preaching and pastoring does go on without driving people into the interdisciplinary encounter does, however, leave the door open for an alternative interpretation, both of Paul and of the operational validity of the conversion message....

If the focus is not, then, on a particular understanding of the individual standing alone and transformed alone, where does it lie? It lies in Jesus' initial proclamation of the imminence of the kingdom. Persons must repent if they are to enter it. Repenting and entering both have subjective dimensions, but they can best be described in terms that include the cognitive (dealing with awareness of ideas) and the social (dealing with the awareness of other persons and groups to which one is related). The description of the change that comes over a person who repents and believes will freely include elements of emotion and self-understanding. But it will not involve any need to demonstrate that the changed nature is self-contained or self-interpreting; nor will it need to demonstrate that its inwardness is prior to, independent of, or the sole and adequate cause of its social reality.

When we move from Jesus to Paul the same answer is more clear. The reconciliation of Jew and Gentile in the "new humanity" is *first* a community event. It *cannot* happen to a lone individual. The prerequisite for personal change is a new context into which people enter. A Gentile can find Abraham only by meeting a Jew. A Jew can celebrate the messianic age only by welcoming a Gentile. This is not to *negate* other dimensions such as mental ideas, psychic self-understandings, feelings, etc. The issue, rather, is the sovereignty of the individualistic definition over other levels of interpretation.

— *To Hear the Word*, 19–21, 26–27

THE INCARNATION AS CRITERION

The infancy narratives in the gospels are not about the baby Jesus but about men and women awaiting the triumphant

Messiah, who were promised suffering instead. Rejection at the inn is followed by Simeon's bitter prophecy, "This child is set for the fall and rising of many in Israel; and for a sign which shall be spoken against (yea, a sword shall pierce through thy own soul also)." Herod's menace fulfills for Matthew Jeremiah's word about Rachel weeping for her children. The peasants for whom, legend says, St. Francis invented the manger scene knew full well that for a child to be born in a barn means for the mother — poverty, stench, and rejection by men, not sweet-smelling hay and cute woolly lambs at play. "Little baby Jesus," clean, chubby, innocent — and in our art usually blond, Aryan — has nothing to do with the gospel. Not the innocence of the infant but the obedience of the person Jesus saves us.

From here it is but a short step to note that what fourth-century Christendom celebrated was not an event but a doctrine, not a life breaking into the world but the miracle of incarnation transforming it. If in the effort to save Christmas we bring to it the full weight of the miracle of God-made-infant, we fall into the docetic heresy, affirming the full divine presence apart from the *story* of the man. Divine sonship is clearly proclaimed first at Jesus' baptism; before that the gospels only point to its promise. For the sake of the real meaning of incarnation, we must, like the gospels, see the cross behind the cradle. It is because that can no longer be done with American Christmas that the time may well have come for surgery.

— "On the Meaning of Christmas," 18–19

Christians are not the propagators of a set of abstract and impersonal principles received "by revelation" and needing to be passed on in a purely verbal form to all who will listen and even hurled at those who do not. Our testimony is not ready-packaged phrases like "Thou shalt love" or "The body is the temple of the Holy Spirit" or "Discrimination is sin." Christians are rather witnesses to a person, to God who in Jesus Christ has become our neighbor and teacher and servant, a person whom we must in every act either confess or disavow, a person whose full humanity must be derived and by whose own personal obedience must be tested every effort to state Christian ethical guidance in terms of "norms" and "principles." Only as descriptions of who he was do our phrases have any substance or any authority.

Jesus Christ is proclaimed by the church as Lord. This is her way of saying that loyalty to him is ultimately effective. And yet it is not within our power to "sight down the line" and to justify the good action we are called to carry out today in terms of the good results we are sure to be able to promise.

The standard by which we measure our obedience is therefore Jesus Christ himself; from him we learn that brokenness, not success, is the normal path of faithfulness to the servanthood of God. This is not to glorify failure or some sort of heroic uselessness, but to claim, as a confession that can be only made in faith, that true "success" in Christian obedience is not to be measured by changing the world in a given direction within a given length of time, but by the congruence between our path and the triumph of Christ.

Every kind of brutal pragmatism down through the centuries has justified itself by the good results; so has every idealistic glorification of whatever anyone is currently doing to save the world. We must relearn the humility of measuring our obedience not by our claims to get something done, which really does not lie in our hands, but rather by its faithfulness to the word that God has spoken to humanity in the person of his choice.

This insistence on the moral priority of the incarnation must be guarded against at least two serious misunderstandings.

A. One traditional way of looking at this problem is the rhetorical contrast between pragmatism and idealism. This assumes that we have a standard of what it means for something to "work," which is itself not subject to moral evaluation, and that on the other hand the "higher" standards being held forth by the "idealist" cannot fully be related to real experience. The meaning of the incarnation is precisely that this dichotomy is not only illogical but that it has been given the lie by the ministry of Jesus.

The paratroopers in Little Rock or the federal marshals in Oxford were meant to be "effective"; yet they froze a conflict situation rather than freeing it. The choice is now between "effective as we figure it out for ourselves" and "effective after the measure of revelation in Christ."

The same would have to be said about such rhetorical polarizations as "love versus justice," or about the way some clothe self-defense or self-affirmation under the label of "love for neighbor" by preferring the interest of the "neighbors" of one's own class or nation to that of "foreign" and "enemy" neighbors. When we insist that Jesus Christ alone is the standard, we are not preferring love to justice or idealism to pragmatism. We are rather confessing Christ as Lord. It is ultimately only the presence of God among men and women which is practical, and it is only love which is really just.

B. The same thing needs to be said about the caricature of Christian discipleship as a search for "purity," as if the most devoted Christians, the strongest critics of violence, or the sharpest adversaries of social injustice were people unwilling to get themselves involved in the dirt and the confusion of everyday reality. Certainly there has been, far too often in Christian history, a Christian search for moral impeccability, but it has not based its claim on an appeal to the example and the experience of Christ, nor is it presently the motor of any social movement, and especially not of nonviolent social action, which is a most involved and confusing way to contribute to social change. The integrity with which Christian ethics is concerned is not the perfection or the innocence of the individual Christian but the welfare of the neighbor. The concern is not for keeping oneself unspotted so much as it is for rigorously refusing to be the cause of the neighbor's suffering.

Identifying with the incarnation as not only the standard but also the motivation and the power for Christian obedience will mean that when exercising a social critique Christians will identify themselves with the "other," the enemy. To the extent to which there is any point in passing out grades of right or wrong, it is evident that the powerful persons in any society are more guilty of injustice. This however does not mean that Christians are able to bless indiscriminately anything done in the interests of redressing the balance between the dominant and the exploited elements in society. When conflict arises, the prime obligation of Christian love is to the enemy. In the present case, considering the vision of "the movement" as we enter the 1960s, the "enemy," insofar as it is a person as distinguished from institutions, is quite evidently frightened Caucasians who hide behind unjust institutions because of their apprehension of what will happen when they lose their privileges. The concern of Christians is not only to identify but also to help change unjust social structures. Yet they are committed to changing them in the way of Christ. This kind of love is more costly in its relation to the agents of evil than in its obvious agreements with those who suffer unjustly. The most costly dimension of the love of Jesus was not his agreement with justified complaints of his oppressed brethren but his willingness to suffer at the hands of the Romans.

The identification of Christ with the poor, the constant theme of Old and New Testament prophetic proclamation, is not understood if we see in it simply a call to upset society and make the poor rich and let the rich take their turn to suffer. The identification of God's suffering servanthood is with people in their suffering; it does not concentrate first on an illusory vision of ending all suffering by a simple shift in the social order, and that is precisely why the change it brings about is real and durable.

It would seem clearly to follow from some of what has been said above that the theological basis for involvement in the non-violent racial revolution, although clear and unambiguous, is not to be too easily identified with the practical and psychological considerations that have driven many others to support the same undertaking.   — *For the Nations*, 108–11

THE IMITATION OF CHRIST

Before drawing any affirmative conclusions let us first note the absence of the concepts of imitation as a *general* pastoral or moral guideline. There is in the New Testament no Franciscan glorification of barefoot itinerancy. Even when Paul argues the case for celibacy, it does not occur to him to appeal to the example of Jesus. Even when Paul explains his own predilection for self-support there is no appeal to Jesus' years as a village artisan. Even when the apostle argues strongly the case for his teaching authority, there is no appeal to the rabbinic ministry of Jesus. Jesus' trade as a carpenter, his association with fishermen, and his choice of illustrations from the life of the sower and the shepherd have throughout Christian history given momentum to the romantic glorification of the handcrafts and the rural life; but there is none of this in the New Testament. It testifies throughout the life and mission of a church going intentionally into the cities in full knowledge of the conflicts that awaited believers there. That the concept of imitation is not applied by the New Testament at some of those points where Franciscan and romantic devotion has tried most piously to apply it, is all the more powerfully a demonstration of how fundamental the thought of participation in the suffering of Christ is when the New Testament church sees it as guiding and explaining her attitude to the powers of the world. Only at one point, only on one subject — but then consistently, universally — is Jesus our example: in his cross. . . .

A long history of interpretation and application that we might designate as "mendicant" has centered its attention on the outward form of Jesus' life: his forsaking domicile and property, his celibacy, or his barefoot itinerancy. Again, without disrespect for the nobility of the monastic tradition and its needed critique of comfortable religion, we must be aware that it centers the renunciation at another point than the New Testament. Both the few who seek thus to follow Jesus in a formal mimicking of his lifestyle and the many who use this distortion to argue Jesus' irrelevance, have failed to note a striking gap in the New Testament material we have read.

As we noted more briefly: there is no *general* concept of living like Jesus in the New Testament. According to universal tradition, Jesus was not married; yet when the apostle Paul, advocate *par excellence* of the life "in Christ," argues at length for celibacy or for a widow's not remarrying (1 Cor. 7), it never occurs to him to appeal to Jesus' example, even as one of many arguments. Jesus is thought in his earlier life to have worked as a carpenter; yet never, even when he explains at length why he earns his own way as an artisan (1 Cor. 9), does it come to Paul's mind that he is imitating Jesus. Jesus' association with villagers, his drawing his illustration from the life of the peasants and the fishermen, his leading his disciples to desert places and mountaintops have often been appealed to as examples by the advocates of rural life and church camping; but not in the New Testament. His formation of a small circle of disciples whom he taught through months of close contact has been claimed as a model pastoral method; his teaching in parables has been made a model of graphic communication; there have been efforts to imitate his prayer life or his forty days in the desert: but we don't find this in the New Testament.

There is but one realm in which the concept of imitation holds — but there it holds in every strand of the New Testament literature and all the more strikingly by virtue of the absence of parallels in other realms. This is at the point of the concrete social meaning of the cross in its relation to enmity and power. Servanthood replaces dominion, forgiveness absorbs hostility. Thus — and only thus — are we bound by New Testament thought to "be like Jesus."

— *The Politics of Jesus*, 95, 130–31

A fundamental critique must then address not merely the space that was made for justifiable violence, but the prior acceptance of the irrelevance of Jesus to the political existence of his disciples, or the prior commitment to the imperative of using the

world's language if we want to challenge the world's imperatives. That is the point at which the sell-out can now be seen to
have occurred. The debate is not about whether the Christian
prohibition of violence might have loopholes. The question is
whether the pertinence of the Jesus story for our present agenda
has to be filtered through some other language and its frame of
reference.

I have in the past said it affirmatively: Jesus is presented by
the gospel writers as a model when he renounces the justifiable insurrection of the Zealots. Now I say it as a critique. A
millennium and a half of efforts to use the more "natural,"
and therefore supposedly more "applicable" categories of the
"just war," is a theme to which Jesus does speak: a perception
for which neither St. Francis nor Tolstoy was yet ready. The
newer urgency of the arms race and of liberation rhetoric frees
a deeper stratum of the gospel. We reconstruct by critiquing and
by remembering.   — *The Priestly Kingdom*, 79

PARTICIPATION IN CHRIST

The claim that the human person has been created "in the image
of God" (however one understands this) means at minimum
that the human person, in what he or she is and does, corre-
sponds to God's own being. This fact of being in God's image is
never debated; it is neither preached nor impressed on people; it
is simply assumed. The basis of the Sabbath command through
a reference to God resting at the completion of creation (Exod.
20) or its basis on the humaneness of God, expressed in the freeing of the enslaved Israelites from Egypt (Exod. 3), makes sense
only when we take into account the correspondence between
God and humanity. "Be holy, for I am holy" (Lev. 11:44) may
well have been a cultic rather than an ethical commandment
at first; nevertheless, a tradition of "following God" attached
itself to this command throughout the prophetic tradition and
through Judaism right up to Martin Buber.

What the Old Testament assumed as a fundamental concept becomes a new reality in the New Testament with the pouring out of the Holy Spirit. "Child of God," "transformed into the image of Christ," "participation in the resurrection," and "in Christ" are expressions describing this new relationship to God, or rather to Christ, and make clear why the Christian is to be no different and to act no different than Christ, a member of whose body the Christian has become. It should be a self-evident implication of this that we should follow Jesus and act as he did with respect to Christ's relationship to evil, just as we do in other matters. This is the viewpoint that is represented, for example, by G. McGregor. Yet the fact that we express this basic claim about which one can speak so edifyingly does not in any way deal with the real need; it merely reveals to us what our need is. The disunity, or for that matter helplessness, of Christians with respect to politics sets in right here. A majority of theologians agree with this general claim but do not allow it to cast any light on the matter of politics. That we are to love the evildoers in the same way God loves them is accepted by these theologians in general, accepted, that is, in the family circle and in other areas of life, but not in terms of the state. That is why it will not suffice to speak about discipleship in general; rather, the question needs to be asked in a much narrower and more difficult form: Does the command to follow Jesus apply for the Christian also in the realm of politics?...

The essence of following Jesus is not grasped if we view it primarily as a commandment to become the same as Jesus, or to act the way Jesus did. Rather following Jesus really means basing our action on our participation in Christ's very being. That is why those who criticize the whole notion of "following Jesus" and who try to make it look ridiculous by asking whether we should not also copy Jesus' singleness, his occupation as a carpenter, or his habit of walking barefoot have missed the point altogether. This is not about some legalistic approach to copying Jesus, but rather about participating in Christ. We are already part of his body; we do not become so through following him. Following Jesus is the result, not the means, of our fellowship with Christ. It is the form of our Christian freedom and not a new law.

—*Discipleship as Political Responsibility*, 51–52, 61

Since Jesus is seen in his full humanity as responding to needs and temptations of a social character, the problems of our obedience to him are not problems in the interpretation of texts. Nor is the question of our fidelity to him one of moralism, a stuffy preoccupation with never making a mistake. The question put to us as we follow Jesus is not whether we have successfully refrained from breaking any rules. Instead, we are asked whether we have been participants in that human experience, that peculiar way of living for God in the world and being used as instruments of the living God in the world, which the Bible calls *agape* or cross.

When we speak of the pacifism of the messianic *community,* we move the focus of ethical concern from the individual to the human community, experiencing in its shared life a foretaste of God's kingdom. Persons may severally and separately ask themselves about right and wrong in their concern for their own integrity. That is fine as far as it goes. The messianic community's experience, however, is different in that it is not a life alone for heroic personalities. Instead, it is a life for a society. It is communal in that it is lived by a covenanting group of men and women who instruct one another, forgive one another, bear one another's burdens, and reinforce one another's witness....

This community resource is not merely a moral crutch or a psychological springboard that enables individuals to feel more free and confident as they take pacifist positions. Even that would be nothing to sneeze at. Being crippled, I am unashamed of needing a crutch, and most of us are moral cripples. Yet the social meaning of a peace witness is far more fundamental than that. The existence of a human community dedicated in common to a new and publicly scandalous enemy-loving way of life is itself a new social datum. A heroic individual can crystallize a widespread awareness of need or widespread admiration.

However, only a continuing community dedicated to a deviant value system can change the world. — *Nevertheless,* 134–36

THE CANON WITHIN THE CANON

The ultimate canon within the canon must in the end . . . be the person of Jesus and, in a broader sense, the narration of the saving acts of God. This follows from the fact that the Bible as a whole corpus of literature is narrative in its framework, although some of its fragments are not. That framework itself dictates the priority of the historical quality over levels of interpretation that would be less historical by being more abstract (such as ontology and systematic dogma) or individualistic.

As Paul Minear indicated long ago, we are most likely to learn from a text something that will constitute genuine learning if we attend to the points at which that text seems to be saying something that we do not already know or have under our control. This is true for any kind of human understanding, whether it be applied to the phenomena of physical or biological nature or to a piece of literature. Even more must it be the case for the Christian scriptures, of which we confess that they testify to us of uniquely revelatory intervention. As the expository ministry of Minear did not cease to illustrate, the points at which we will most likely learn will therefore not be those already previously reduced to a rational system, but rather the odd, forgotten, or systemically erratic blocks within the literature. . . .

It is most lively and productive to think of one body of literature, the Bible, representing in any time and place the testimony of the narrative stretching from Abraham to the apostles, which can be juxtaposed to any other age by its psalms being sung again, its letters being read again, its stories and parables being retold. Then in the juxtaposition of those stories with our stories there leaps the spark of the Spirit, illuminating parallels and contrasts, to give us the grace to see our age in God's light and God's truth in our words. This picture of how it works is more representative of the experienced facts, but also more rigorous than the classical scholastic vision of an unchanging body of timeless propositions needing to be twisted to fit a new age by the special skills of rationalistic linguists....

In the spiral movement whereby the mind of the church constantly links the world's agenda and the canonical texts, one does find a degree of progress in any given context in becoming clearer both about what it is in the present challenge to which scripture speaks and about what the answer is. This growing clarity cannot be imposed on other times and places, but we do learn about some of the priorities in our time and place if we keep the circuit open. That the God of the Bible cares about the future of this earth and the human race, rather than intending to leave it behind as a radioactive cinder in order for disembodied souls to enjoy themselves timelessly in a placeless heaven, is a truth that grows on anyone who reads the scriptures with that question in mind, even though for centuries it was possible for readers not to notice that testimony, so thoroughly had they been taken in by neo-Platonism....

We are used to being told, over against a timeless platonic message of truths unrelated to time and place, that we should rejoice that God chose to be revealed through the particular. The incarnation does not mean that humankind in general, or human nature in general, or human history in general was stamped with God's approval or transformed by God's indwelling, but rather that a particular story, the words and work of a particular person, is the key to the very nature of God. That particularity is even more scandalous if we reckon deeply with the fact that the historicity of the incarnation committed God to the particularity of an ongoing history. God entrusted the incarnational disclosure not only to a first generation of witnesses to the person Jesus, but also to the necessarily ensuing chain of specific bodies of tradition-bearing, fallible people who through the centuries would unfold and distort the message. It is not a regrettable mistake of church strategy contrary to the divine plan when we find ourselves needing to deal with the unfinished quality of the definition of the Christian story.   — To Hear the Word, 77–79, 83, 97

One of the marks of the "believers' church" heritage is that it sees movement within the canonical story and therefore a difference between the testaments. Instead of a timeless collection of parabolic anecdotes for allegorical application, or of propositional communications ready for deductive exposition, the Bible is a story of promise and fulfillment that must be read directionally. The New Testament, by affirming the Hebrew scriptures, which Christians have come to call the Old Testament, also interprets them. Abraham and Moses are read through Jesus and Paul....

Far from being an ongoing growth like a tree (or a family tree), the wholesome growth of a tradition is like a vine: a story of constant interruption of organic growth in favor of pruning and a new chance for the roots. This renewed appeal to origins is not primitivism, nor an effort to recapture some pristine purity. It is rather a "looping back," a glance over the shoulder to enable a midcourse correction, a rediscovery of something from the past whose pertinence was not seen before, because only a new question or challenge enables us to see it speaking to us. To stay with the vinedresser's image, the effect of pruning is not to harm the vine, but to provoke new growth out of the old wood nearer to the ground, to decrease the loss of food and time along the sap's path from roots to fruit, and to make the grapes easier to pick. *Ecclesia reformata semper reformanda* is not really a statement about the church. It is a statement about the earlier tradition's permanent accessibility, as witnessed to and normed by scripture at its nucleus, but always including more dimensions than the Bible itself contains, functioning as an instance of appeal as we call for renewed faithfulness and denounce renewed apostasy. The most important operational meaning of the Bible for ethics is not that we do just what it says in some way that we can derive deductively. It is rather that we are able, thanks to the combined gifts to teachers and prophets, to become aware that we do not do what it says and that the dissonance we thereby create enables our renewal.

There is no reproach involved when we affirm this need for correction. Sometimes a need for correction is the result of culpable failure or disobedience. Sometimes it is the result of not having listened or waited. Yet often the need for continuing historical correction is blameless, intrinsic to the quality of historically rooted community. We should feel guilty not when we need to be corrected but when we claim to bypass that need, as if our link to our origins were already in our own hands.

What we then find at the heart of our tradition is not some proposition, scriptural or promulgated otherwise, that we hold to be authoritative and to be exempt from the relativity of hermeneutical debate by virtue of its inspiredness. What we find at the origin is already a process of reaching back again to the origins, to the earliest memories of the event itself, confident that that testimony, however intimately integrated with the belief of the witnesses, is not a wax nose and will serve to illuminate and sometimes adjudicate our present path.

—*The Priestly Kingdom*, 9, 69–70

THE SCANDAL OF
THE APOSTOLIC WITNESS

There are also dimensions of the apostolic witness, especially if we let the apostles remind us of the centrality of the cross, that are less attractive. I ought to name three of those "scandal" factors; they overlap.

1. In words that all three synoptic gospels use (each in a different setting), Jesus called his followers to follow him in renouncing dominion in favor of servanthood. In our own culture, as in most others, self-esteem is linked with "empowerment" and dignity with "leadership" or "autonomy." Some argue that the servant is the best leader, or even the most powerful leader, even in government or industry, but it is a paradoxical point and most of us do not believe it, including those of us who are presently servants.

2. The point at which the Sermon on the Mount focused most clearly the intensification of the law, which the heralding of the coming kingdom enables, is that, like our heavenly Father and like Jesus himself (although our imitating Jesus is not the theme of the sermon), we are not to answer evil with evil but to love our enemies. For since Augustine, theologians have invested great ingenuity in dulling the edge of that call. Ever since Tolstoy at the beginnings of modernity, honest readers have had to admit that that is what Jesus meant, even when they do not intend to follow it. Loving the enemy is one good candidate for the status of a moral imperative specific to Christianity, or to Jesus, which I was asking about at the outset, if there is such a phenomenon within ethics (although, for reasons I alluded to earlier, I am not preoccupied with disengaging the distinctiveness of Christianity).

3. One simple yet central component of viable community is forgiveness. Forgiving frees all the parties to the social nexus from the retaliatory mechanisms that lie at the bottom of cultural evolution. Forgiveness is a part of the process of "binding and loosing." ... It is the only social process referred to in the prayer Jesus taught us. As independent a social philosopher as Hannah Arendt has identified it as the necessary condition for a society's ability to survive.

   The retaliatory imperative is at the heart of numerous of our society's current debates, as (alone among the industrialized nations) we in the United States escalate the punitiveness of our criminal justice system. Civil justice as well is increasingly punitive, as we have recently seen in judgments against McDonald's when spilled coffee is too hot and against Exxon when spilled oil is too dirty. From Cain and Lamech in Genesis 4 to the sociologist Durkheim to the cultural philosopher René Girard to the fifty new capital offenses in President Clinton's new federal crime bill, the theme of tit-for-tat punishment is the key to understanding the pathology of how we live together.

Killing the killer is the standard response. Killing a scape-
goat instead of the killer is, according to René Girard, the
improved response that makes viable civilization possible.
Forgiveness is one way to connect the death of the scape-
goat to the offenses that keep being committed, but as our
national experience demonstrates, most of us consider it
unacceptable.

These three strands join in one holistic, Christological, paradigmatic proclamation: servanthood, enemy love, forgiveness. If
we are interested in making sense to our unbelieving or otherwise-
believing neighbors, let this threefold cord be the test case.

Let those who fear sectarian self-sufficiency and seek "public" relevance show us how they can articulate — in reasonable
discourse describing the nature of things so that all our neighbors will come along — the relevance and the realism of
servanthood, enemy love, and forgiveness. This, and not domination, ethnocentricity, and punishment, is the divinely given
nature of things that we are called to show the world.

Let those on the other hand who fear selling out, whether to
the liberal or the conservative versions of establishment, those
who prefer to locate the community's dissenting integrity only
internally, show us how their tactical distancing from mainstream
conformities heightens the clarity with which these three strands
of fidelity are manifested to the watching and waiting world.

Most of the time when the apostle Paul was writing about
Jews and Greeks, his concern was with their reconciliation.
Yet we do have one weighty passage where they are named as
characterizing two kinds of unbelief, namely, near the beginning of his first letter to the Corinthians. Jews, Paul tells us,
are concerned for self-authenticating signs, and the cross in its
apparent weakness causes them to stumble. Greeks are concerned for wisdom, and to them the cross looks foolish. I
suggest that to juxtapose this passage with our present theme
may be illuminating.

The "communitarians" of our time, for whom all meaning
is internally self-authenticating, may be taken to stand for the

people whom Paul in this passage calls "Jews." They will not risk the challenge of telling the world that servanthood, enemy love, and forgiveness would be a better way to run a university, a town, or a factory. They pull back on the grounds that only they have already experienced the power and novelty of that threefold evangelical cord in the worship and ministry of the church. They affirm integrity but at the cost of witness.

The "public catholics" on the other hand are like Paul's "Greeks." They are concerned not to look foolish to their sophisticated neighbors by making any claims or promises linked to the particularity of the Jew Jesus (or of their own denominational past). By dropping the particular baggage of normative servanthood, enemy love, and forgiveness, they think they might make it easy to get across Lessing's ditch and to talk their neighbors' language, but they do so at the cost of having nothing to say that the neighbors do not already know.

Paul's stance in the face of this bifocal challenge is not so much "neither of the above" as "both." Being himself eminently both "Jew" and "Greek," he affirms both identity and intelligibility not as poles of a zero-sum trade-off, so that more of one means less of the other, but as each being the necessary condition of the other, each being pointless without the other.

...I make no brief for the exhaustiveness of these listings. I do make a brief for the aptness of the shape of my synthesis. Because the risen Messiah is at once head of the church and *kyrios* of the *kosmos,* sovereign of the universe, what is given to the church through him is in substance no different from what is offered to the world. The believing community is the new world on the way.   —*For the Nations,* 47–50

THE LAMB AND
THE MEANING OF HISTORY

John, on the island of Patmos, wept because no one was able to unseal the scroll that he saw in the hand of the one seated on the throne. To translate, no one could explain the meaning of

the history in which John and his fellow believers found themselves, still oppressed three generations after Pentecost. Then he
saw on the scene a figure who had not been there before: the
"Lamb" bearing the signs of his having been slain. Then he
heard the heavenly creatures and the whole universe break into
"a new song," a song that could not have been sung before,
rejoicing that the Lamb was "worthy to receive power, because
by his blood he was purchasing for God people of every tribe
and tongue and nation." To translate, the meaning of history
is the reconciling work of the church. The meaning of history
is not carried by Caesars and Cromwells, military liberators
ancient or modern, as much as by the creation of a new human
fellowship through the cross, defined precisely by transcend-
ing enmity between classes of people. This does not make our
efforts to understand the fallen world systematically and to contribute as we can to relative justice and liberation unimportant.
This does not render our refusal to collaborate in unjust systems and our conscientious and costly participation in relatively
more just systems, despite their imperfection, unimportant. It
does deny to us either a need or a right to so glorify our passing
human systems that we would arrogate to ourselves the authority to destroy our fellow human beings in the name of any such
cause....

   If it should be the case that Jesus is more politically relevant than had long been thought or that the apostolic vision
of the historical process is more realistic than was thought,
then that will not be merely a corrective on the formal level
concerning how seriously to take certain ancient texts. It also
becomes a new perspective on the appropriateness of the nonviolent morality that we had been told was outmoded. Thus
the more empathetic vision of the scriptures as our still-living
canon has more to tell us than the "realism" that claims to be
describing the only choices permitted by the world around us
but that, in truth, has less to say about fallenness and hope than
the apostles.   — *Nonviolence*, 104–5

2

The Mandate of the Church

As we have already seen, Yoder acknowledges that a heroic individual is useful for crystallizing a widespread awareness of need or for creating widespread admiration. Yet this is an accurate description of neither Yoder's Jesus nor his normative Christianity. In Yoder's analysis, Christianity changed (and continues to change) the world. Accomplishing this task requires more than individuals; it requires a "continuing community dedicated to a deviant value system" (see above p.57). This, for Yoder, is the church, the body of Christ.

To begin to illuminate his multivalent reflections on the church, this second series of readings opens with a brief orienting summary of the ways in which God works in history, both visibly and invisibly. Working against what he perceives to be a persistent misunderstanding of the church, Yoder argues that God works visibly in the world through the church and, therefore, the meaning of history lies in the creation and work of the church.

If the first reading roughly sketches the importance of the church, the next five readings further develop Yoder's definition of the church as a new pattern of relationships and attitudes that reveal a new vision of what it means to be a human being or, described from another direction, as a new expression of communal discipleship or faithfulness in following Jesus. As much as the church exists for its own sake first, its existence is also a proclamation, a witness. To explain how Yoder *believes these notions cohere, the next four readings elucidate how Yoder's church proclaims the gospel in and through its very existence as a doxological community.*

Finally, the remaining six readings conclude this series in a more critical vein as they outline several unfaithful paths that remain temptations for the church alongside several means of avoiding these temptations, including the appropriate use of theologians and the importance of remembering the Jewish nature of the church. Once Yoder's vision of how God works visibly in history through the church is firmly in view, we are prepared to turn to the next section, which includes Yoder's pregnant gestures in the direction of how God works in history outside of the church.

GOD'S WAY OF WORKING IN HISTORY

According to the New Testament witness, God works in history on two distinguishable levels.

The church is a visible, confessing community. Its celebration is visible. Its confession is public. Its lifestyle differs from that of its neighbors, and the neighbors know it. This voluntary minority body is an organ of the work of God in history. People know where to go to find the church; they know what Christians do and how they differ from those who are not believers.

God also works invisibly to govern the world, through the fact that the risen Christ is at the right hand of the Father. "Sitting at the right hand" of the ruler is ancient language identifying the function of the prime minister, the one who makes the kingdom run. The risen Christ at the right hand of the Father governs the universe. Christians cannot always see how God is ruling the world, especially in times of persecution. They cannot immediately see that events in secular history or in cultural history have been providentially governed so that things come out in a certain way, but the early church confesses a hidden meaning and a meaning that believers can know sometimes through the prophets and sometimes through experience and discernment. Thus the risen Lord uses the powers, including the economic and political powers, despite themselves, for his hidden purposes.

In short, New Testament Christians knew for a fact that God uses the church for ministries of proclamation, service, and fellowship, but they had to take it on faith that God governs the world.

Eusebius's understandings. After Constantine, this faith fundamentally changed. Eusebius and Augustine, the two great minds of the fourth and early fifth centuries, worked out an alternative: God governs history through Constantine. In their interpretation, what Constantine did went far beyond granting Christians religious liberty. More profoundly, Constantine became for Eusebius a kind of savior, bishop, and theologian. Eusebius made the empire into the church, and the barbarian outsider became the infidel, the nonbeliever. In this visible order of God's work in history it was only fitting that there not be liberty for non-Christians or even for dissenting Christians.

— *Christian Attitudes to War, Peace,*
and Revolution, 61–62

DISCIPLESHIP AND
THE CHURCH AS WITNESS

Jesus made it clear that the nationalized hope of Israel had been a misunderstanding and that God's true purpose was the creation of a new society, unidentifiable with any of the local, national, or ethnic solidarities of any time. This new body, the church, as aftertaste of God's loving triumph on the cross and foretaste of his ultimate loving triumph in his kingdom, has a task within history. History is the framework in which the church evangelizes, so that the true meaning of history is the fact that God has chosen to use it for such a "scaffolding" service....

In spite of the present visible dominion of the "powers" of "this present evil age," the triumph of Christ has already guaranteed that the ultimate meaning of history will not be found in the course of earthly empires or the development of proud cultures, but in the calling together of the "chosen race, royal priesthood, holy nation," which is the church of Christ. The church is not fundamentally a source of moral stimulus to encourage the development of a better society — though a faithful church should also have this effect — it is for the sake of the church's own work that society continues to function. The meaning of history — and therefore the significance of the state — lies in the creation and the work of the church. The reason for Christian prayer in favor of the political authorities is that "God our Savior desires all men to be saved and to come to the knowledge of the truth" (1 Tim. 2:3–5). The function of the state in maintaining an ordered society is thereby a part of the divine plan for the evangelization of the world....

The first level of the church's faithfulness and, in a sense, the test of the validity of everything else she shall say later, will be her own obedience to the standards of discipleship. If it is clear to the church, as it was in New Testament times, that the central meaning of history is borne not by kings and empires but by the church herself, then her first duty to society will be the same as her first duty to her Lord. Her witness to the primacy of her faith will be visible in evangelistic activity (in the traditional, restricted sense of that term, a usage itself open to challenge), but just as fundamentally in the service of the needy and equally in her refusal to use means unfitting to her ends. What we say here of the church is valid for individual Christians as well. They will not permit their local obligations to one particular state to lead them to treat in an unbrotherly way an enemy of that state. An attempt, for example, to justify war for the individual Christian citizen, after it has been judged incompatible with the ministry of the church, is a refusal to be honest with the absolute priority of church over state in the plan of God.

The church is herself a society. Her very existence, the fraternal relations of her members, their ways of dealing with their differences and their needs are, or rather should be, a demonstration of what love means in social relations. This demonstration cannot be transposed directly into non-Christian society, for in the church it functions only on the basis of repentance and faith; yet by analogy certain of its aspects may be instructive as stimuli to the conscience of society. For the church and the reign of Christ will one day be englobed in the same kingdom. That kingdom will mean the victory of the church and the overcoming of the world; as anticipation of that consummation it is possible for the potentially victorious order to testify to the potentially vanquished order concerning the absolute norm that is valid for both and in contradiction to which the world will never succeed in building even a stable temporal order.

— *The Christian Witness to the State,* 10–11, 13, 16–17

THE ORIGINAL REVOLUTION

When he called his society together, Jesus gave its members a new way of life to live. He gave them a new way to deal with offenders — by forgiving them. He gave them a new way to deal with violence — by suffering. He gave them a new way to deal with money — by sharing it. He gave them a new way to deal with problems of leadership — by drawing upon the gift of every member, even the most humble. He gave them a new way to deal with a corrupt society — by building a new order, not smashing the old. He gave them a new pattern of relationships between man and woman, between parent and child, between master and slave, in which was made concrete a radical new vision of what it means to be a human person. He gave them a new attitude toward the state and toward the "enemy nation." ...

All of this new peoplehood — the being-together with one another and the being different in style of life — his disciples freely promised to do, as he renewed the promise that through them the world should be blessed and turned rightside up.

Now the usual name for this new society that Jesus created is "church." But when we use the word "church" in our day we mean by it a gathering for worship, or the group of persons who gather for worship, or who might so gather, and who otherwise have little to do with each other. Sometimes it even means the building they meet in, or the organization that provides that there will be an officiant at the meeting, or even the national agency that manages the pension fund for the officiants' widows. But the word that Jesus used in the Aramaic language, like the equivalent word that the New Testament writers used in the Greek language, does not mean a gathering for worship nor an administration; it means a public gathering to deal with community business. Our modern terms "assembly," "parliament," "town meeting," are the best equivalents. The church is not just a certain number of persons nor a specific gathering of persons assembled for a particular religious rite. The church is God's people gathered as a unit, as a people, gathered to do business in his name, to find what it means here and now to put into practice this different quality of life that is God's promise to them and to the world and their promise to God and service to the world.

Jesus did not bring to faithful Israel any corrected ritual or any new theories about the being of God. He brought them a new peoplehood and a new way of living together. The very existence of such a group is itself a deep social change. Its very presence was such a threat that he had to be crucified. But such a group is not only by its existence a novelty on the social scene; if it lives faithfully, it is also the most powerful tool of social change.   — *The Original Revolution*, 29, 30–31

LET THE CHURCH BE THE CHURCH

In the slogan "Let the church be the church," which has been so sorely overworked in recent times, there is a paradox that is not only grammatical. The form of this call, "become what you are," is true to the New Testament pattern of thought. Often the apostle Paul, following a ringing proclamation of what it means to be a Christian, to be "in Christ," then continues with an imperative, "Let this be true of you." "Did you not die with Christ?" the apostle appeals, "Then put to death those parts of you which belong to the earth" (Col. 2:20; 3:5). After declaring that Christians have been made one (Eph. 2; 3), Paul continues with the appeal to them to act according to this call.

The call to "become what we are" means on the one hand that we are not being asked anything unnatural, anything impossible by definition. The summons is simply to live up to what a Christian — or the church — is when confessing that Christ is Lord.

And yet at the same time this imperative says negatively, "You are not what you claim to be." The church is not, fully and genuinely, all of what it means to be the church; otherwise we should not have to be called on to become that reality that in Christ we are supposed to be. We have been giving our attention to being something other than the church. It is from this lack of clear dedication to our major cause that we need to be called to cease trying to do something else and to become what we are.

What then is the church and what should it be? One source will tell us that it is "one, holy, catholic, and apostolic"; another will tell us that it is to be found "where the sacraments are properly administered and the Word of God is properly preached." Still others would test the moral performance or the intensity of piety that can be seen in individual members. But in our age there is arising with new clarity an understanding that what it means to be the church must be found in a clearer grasp of relation to what is not the church, namely, "the world."

For us to say with the current ecumenical fashion that the church is a witnessing body, a serving body, and a body fellowshiping voluntarily and visibly is to identify it thrice as not being the same thing as the total surrounding society. This definition demands for the church an existence, a structure, a sociology of its own, independent of the other structures of society. It can no longer be simply what "church" has so long meant in Europe, that administrative division of civil government that arranges to have preachers in the pulpits, nor can it be what is so often true in America, one more service club, which, even though it has many members registered, still needs to compete with other loyalties for their time and attention.

— *The Royal Priesthood,* 169–70

In all of humanity's effort to understand its experience people have been prone to polarize. Christians have traditionally distinguished between the visible church and the invisible church, between the spirit and the body, between the ordained and the laity, between love and justice. We may now come to see that a more useful and more biblical distinction would be one that does not try to distinguish between realms of reality like body and spirit or the visible and the invisible, nor between categories defined by ritual (lay and ordained), or by abstraction (love and justice), but rather between the basic personal postures of persons, some of whom confess and others of whom do not confess that Jesus Christ is Lord. The distinction between church and the world is not something that God has imposed upon the world by a prior metaphysical definition, nor is it only something that timid or Pharisaical Christians have built up around themselves. It is all of that in creation that has taken the freedom not yet to believe....

The pattern of faithfulness is one of genuine obedience in human experience — which we may well call incarnation. But it is always also a break with the continuities of human civilization and the loyalties of local human societies, which we call election or exodus. When we then speak of incarnation it must not mean God's sanctifying our society and our vocations as they are, but rather his reaching into human reality to say what we must do and what we must leave behind. Not all of life is to be blessed; not all human efforts can be penetrated by the glow of divine indwelling. In a world not yet the kingdom of Christ, it is through the initiative of incarnation that we can trace the reality of human obedience. Yet that obedience, at the same time that it is truly human, is also clearly different from the world around us. *God's pattern of Incarnation is that of Abraham and not of Constantine....*

The alternative to Constantine was Abraham, father of the faithful. And what was the posture of Abraham? Or of Moses? That of the prophet who was listened to by only a minority. To recognize that the church is a minority is not a statistical but a theological observation. It means our convinced acceptance of the fact that we cannot oblige the world to hold the faith that is the basis of our obedience, and therefore we should not expect of the world that kind of moral performance which would appropriately be the fruit of our faith. *Therefore,* our vision of obedience cannot be tested by whether we can ask it of everyone.   — *The Original Revolution,* 109–10, 112, 116

We have asked whether the New Testament provides any concept with which it would be possible to interpret the structures and the history of a secular society. In the Pauline understanding of the powers we have discovered a line of thought very apt to deal with this kind of matter.

In this view of things the condition of the creature, our fallen state, the continual providential care of God, which preserves us as human, the saving work of Christ, and the specific position of the Christian community in the midst of history are all described in terms of social structure and their inherent dynamics. Thus there can easily be established a correlation with contemporary ways of understanding society and history. This in turn drives us to suggest that we can describe more specifically the place of the church within the larger society.

For Paul, as interpreted by Berkhof, the very existence of the church is its primary task. It is in itself a proclamation of the lordship of Christ to the powers from whose dominion the church has begun to be liberated. The church does not attack the powers; this Christ has done. The church concentrates on not being seduced by them. By existing, the church demonstrates that their rebellion has been vanquished.

This Pauline vision of the place of the church in the world bears decisive implications for the contemporary ecumenical

discussion of the place of the church in a world in the midst of
rapid social change. The phrase "responsible society" became
very current since its occurrence in the preparatory documents
for the Amsterdam Assembly of 1948. In these documents it
was strongly affirmed that if the church is to have a ministry to
society in general, the first step of this duty is toward its own
identity. "Let the church be the church," was the slogan. "Let
the church be a restored society," we could have said equally
well. The church must be a sample of the kind of humanity
within which, for example, economic and racial differences are
surmounted. Only then will it have anything to say to the society that surrounds it about how those differences must be dealt
with. Otherwise preaching to the world a standard of reconciliation that is not its own experience will be neither honest nor
effective.   — *The Politics of Jesus,* 149–51

THE IMPORTANCE OF UNITY
IN DISCIPLINED DISCIPLESHIP

The New Testament and the witness of the Anabaptists seem
to agree that it is the duty of the evangelical Christian to seek
to establish and maintain brotherly relationships with anyone
who confesses Christ. They agree further that "brotherly relationships" means much more than is generally understood; they
require not only polite mutual recognition or even "intercom-
munion" (the term used in ecumenical circles for the mutual
acceptance, by two denominations, of the validity of each other's
sacraments); brotherly relations meant, to both the New Testament and the Anabaptists, unity in disciplined discipleship —
something much more difficult to attain than the mere mutual
recognition of separate denominations. Unity does not mean that
we approve of the present belief and behavior of another Christian; it means that we lay upon him the claims that Christ lays
upon those who confess his name; we ask of him Christian obedience, biblical baptism, separation from the world, and the rest
of what the gospel implies.

If there is to be a breach in fellowship between us, that breach cannot be at our initiative. If the fellow Christian with whom we discuss is willing to "return the compliment" and to lay upon us, according to his convictions, the claims that Christ lays upon his disciples, we must converse with him. If our concepts of Christ's claims are different, even contradictory, that means we must keep on conversing and appealing to scripture, and that there will be little that we can usefully do together in a practical way beyond keeping up our conversation; but as long as his convictions are sincere and he is willing to admit scripture as our court of appeal, we have no right to take the initiative in breaking off relations with him. He can, however, take the initiative, in a number of ways; he can, for instance, make it clear that for him there are other authorities besides the Bible that are binding. With Roman Catholics, Adventists, Jehovah's Witnesses, Christian Scientists, and Mormons, this additional authority is so clear that the possibility of real conversation is practically nil. We may well come to the point where conversation is no longer possible because of certain postulates, not scriptural in origin, that the other party refuses to let be called into question. This may happen, for instance, in the case of theological liberals, for whom a modest philosophy or a certain view of science or history is not open to question; or in the case of some orthodox Lutherans, for whom a person always remains first of all a sinner, and the state is fully autonomous in its own realm. It may also be that, for reasons not in our control, the other party will refuse to accept our good faith. In such cases we must accept, reluctantly, and only for a time, the break.

The other point at which fellowship can be broken is the point where, without contesting the rightness of the claims we lay upon him, someone simply decides not to obey. This is the normal situation foreseen in Matthew 18; it calls for successive appeals to repentance and reconciliation but may eventually come to excommunication. Once again, even though the excommunication is pronounced by the church, the initial breach of fellowship was the responsibility of the unfaithful individual.

It would be wrong to leave this analysis without the reminder that the above paragraphs have made one unjustified assumption. They have assumed that "we" are right and "they," the other Christians with whom we converse, are wrong. If we face honestly the fact that this assumption is only theoretical, and that in fact "we" have something to learn just as surely as we have something to teach, then the need for conversation becomes all the more clear.

The extent to which it may be possible to do things together will depend entirely upon the degree of agreement already reached. Less unity is needed to converse than to commune; less unity is needed to evangelize together than to baptize together; less to advocate morality than to apply discipline; less to attack liberalism together than to agree together on what is sound doctrine. The essential for obedience in this realm is to go neither farther nor less far than existing agreement permits. If we refuse to converse because we cannot commune, we fail to go the first mile (to say nothing of the second) toward restoration of fellowship, as did the apostle Paul and the Anabaptists. If, on the other hand, we commune where there is actually only sufficient unity for conversing, we cheapen both unity and truth and do our brother no good.

— *The Ecumenical Movement and the Faithful Church,* 35–38

THE HERMENEUTIC ROLE
OF THE COMMUNITY

Thus the question "How does scripture work to order and reorder?" is transmuted into the question, "What shape ought the believing community have in order for the Word thus to work?" It would need to be a community that disavowed the Solomonic or Constantinian vision of giving the civil community no choice. It would need to be a community whose very self-definition is its corporate aptness for the hermeneutic task.

It would need to be a community committed to the ministry of "first fruits," prefiguring in its own life the kingdom reality to which the whole world is called. This is the type of community sociologically characterized as "baptist."

If scripture were a systematized compendium of final answers, to be applied with compelling deductive logic to all future settings, then the person to do it would be the most learned master of the texts, or of deductive logic. If, however, our guide is a repertory of more or less pertinent paradigms, needing to be selected and transformed transculturally in ever new settings, no one person can monopolize that process. It must be carried by the entire believing community, joining complementarily those who are most authentically part of the local setting with those who best represent the worldwide community and the canonical memories.

This hermeneutic role of the community is thus primordial, i.e., we have to talk about it first. It is, however, by no means an exclusive possession, especially not in the post-Christian global culture. The question "Is this something only Christians can say?" is pointless in this setting. When the empirical community becomes disobedient, other people can hear the Bible's witness too. It is after all a public document. Loners and outsiders can hear it speaking, especially if the insiders have ceased to listen. It was thanks to the loner Tolstoy and the outsider Gandhi that the churchman Martin Luther King Jr., with his Boston personalist education was able to bring Jesus' word on violence back into the churches. It was partly the outsider Marx who has enabled liberation theologians to restate what the law and the prophets had been saying for centuries, largely unheard, about God's partisanship for the poor.   — *For the Nations,* 92–93

COMMUNICATING THE GOOD NEWS

Evangelism means to say and to believe that it is *good news.* But is it not true that most of us have thought otherwise? Among many peace church Christians a different set of assumptions is at work. We tend to assume that the central evangelistic message is good news and is free with no questions asked. First get forgiveness and love and peace of soul. Then you begin to follow Jesus. Then comes the fine print, the hard part, the next step.

You may have learned to talk about this "next step" as a process of nurture or sanctification that you have to work at. Or you may have been taught that it will come automatically, that it is a by-product of the faith. In any case, we have been taught that this further step or further process, the demands of the gospel, will be more clear if the two steps are held apart. The moreness of the gospel life is the second step, the hard one, the bad news that comes after the good news.

This is not what Jesus says. He says it is all good news. He says it is by grace through faith that peacemakers are the children of God, and that is a joyful message because it is part of the kingdom coming. That those who hunger and thirst for righteousness shall be filled is *good news,* because the kingdom is at hand.

The same point is evident from another side as well. We live in a society that largely claims to be Christian, with chaplains in the armed forces and in the houses of Congress, with school prayer amendments in the Congress, with godly slogans on our money and postage stamps. And yet no *one* church is official. The result of this is the assumption that there are two levels to being Christian. One is the basics, the common denominator, the agreed minimum requirement. This is what it takes to be Christian, or to be a Christian; and then there are the additional options, the folkloric furbelows:

- The Anglicans add bishops.
- The Baptists add more water.
- The Wesleyans add holiness.
- The evangelicals add correct doctrine.
- The Pentecostals add spirit.
- The peace churches add their thing.

All of these options, added to the basic minimum of the Protestant cultural heritage, are called "distinctives." It is considered good to have them, but they are not fundamental. The automobile dealer would call them pizzazz. The sociologist will call them folklore. They add character and individuality and taste, but they don't really matter.

Once you understand things this way, which of the levels is the gospel? Is it the minimum requirement? Or is it the more, the second mile?

Some of us have obviously tended to assume the former. The gospel is the minimum to which more will be added. The gospel is the common American Protestant message, which is more acceptable and more essential and more powerful if we leave off the options when presenting it.

But Jesus seems to be saying it the other way around. For him the distinctives identify the gospel. Evangelism, good news, is proclaiming precisely the plus, the otherness, the moreness, the nonconformity of the church as a visible city on a hill. It is the savor of the salt. It is the greater righteousness that fulfills the law, which people see and glorify our heavenly Father.

The plus quality of the life according to the gospel is more than a *result* of the gospel. It is more than a *verification* or confirmation of the gospel. It is also the *communication* of the gospel. It is evangelism. It is the distinctives, in fact, that identify the message.

Jesus is not saying, "Be good, be different, be nonconformed, and people will see how good you are. They will want to have what you have." No, their attention, according to the passage, is drawn not to us but to the Father. Yet attention is drawn to the Father, not by a new set of words, but by a new kind of life.

We must be careful. The differentness that attracts people is not just any old differentness, not just a "Hey, look!" symbolic call for attention. The distinctiveness Jesus is talking about is not like a Salvation Army uniform or a clergyman's collar, or plain garb, which tells you "here is somebody set apart," but does not tell you why or how they differ. The differentness with Jesus, the differentness that says something, is itself the message.

If I am the child of a Father who loves both good and evil children, if I am witness for a God who loves his enemies, then when I love my enemy I am *proclaiming* that love. I am not just obeying it; I am communicating it. And I cannot communicate it any other way.

The enemy whom I love, the person coercing me with whom I go a second mile, experiences through me the call to accept grace, because my action makes God's forgiveness real. No other way could do that.

If I lovingly go the second mile or turn the other cheek to someone who struck me, I am speaking God's forgiving love in the form of the situation by standing before him defenseless.

So it would be with the rest of the Sermon on the Mount. If, as Jesus calls us to do, we forsake our goods to follow him, we are proclaiming our trust in a Father who knows our needs. If, as he tells us to do, we tell the truth without varnish, without oaths and asseverations, we proclaim the sanctity of the name of God and of truthfulness. If, as he tells us to, we forsake self-defense, we preach that Christ, and not the ruler with the biggest army, is the Lord of history.

—*He Came Preaching Peace*, 50–52

THE PROCLAMATION
OF COMMUNITY

The centrality of the church in God's purposes is stated in a figurative way in the first vision of the Apocalypse, where the question of the meaning of history is represented to the seer in the form of a sealed scroll. When it is announced that the Lamb that was slain is worthy to open the seals and unroll the meaning of history, the "new song" in which all the heavenly creatures join proclaims that the meaning of the sacrifice of the Lamb is that he has "purchased" "for God" a priestly kingdom out of "every tribe and language and people and nation" (5:9–10).

Almost the same language is used in the sermonic context of 1 Peter 2, where the phrase "priestly kingdom" finds its counterpart, "royal priesthood," in addition to three other parallel collective nouns describing the church as a people claimed by God. Here "having received mercy" and "being a people," after having been "not a people," are synonymous.

The same statement is made more systematically in Ephesians. Here the apostle claims to have been given understanding of a mystery hidden not only through the ages but also to the other apostles, which has been revealed first of all in his ministry and then in his understanding of that ministry. The creation of one new humanity by breaking down the wall between the two kinds of people of whom the world is made, Jews and Gentiles, is not simply the result of reconciliation of individuals with God, nor is it an ad hoc organization established to support the propagation of the knowledge of individual reconciliation. This creation of the one new humanity is itself the purpose that God had in all ages, is itself the "mystery," the gospel now to be proclaimed.

In every direction we might follow in exposition, *the distinctness of the church of believers is prerequisite to the meaningfulness of the gospel message.* If what is called "the church" is the religious establishment of a total society, then the announcement that God has created human community is redundant, for the religiously sanctioned community is identical with the given order. The identification of the church with a given society denies the miracle of the new humanity in two ways: on the one hand by blessing the existing social unity and structure that is a part of the fallen order rather than a new miracle, and on the other hand by closing its fellowship to those of the outside or the enemy class or tribe or people or nation. If any concept of meaningful mission is to remain in this context, it must be transmuted to the realm of subjectivity, calling a few individuals to a depth of "authenticity" that separates them from their brethren.

Pragmatically it is self-evident that there can be no procedure of proclamation without a community, distinct from the rest of society, to do the proclaiming. Pragmatically it is just as clear that there can be no evangelistic call addressed to people inviting them to enter into a new kind of fellowship and learning if there is not such a body of persons, again distinct from the totality of society, to whom to come and from whom to learn. But this congruence between the free visible existence of the believers' church and the possibility of valid missionary proclamation is not a merely pragmatic or instrumental one. It is founded deeply in the nature of the gospel itself. If it is not the case that there are in a given place people of various characters and origins who have been brought together in Jesus Christ, then there is not in that place the new humanity and in that place the gospel is not true. If, on the other hand, this miracle of new creation has occurred, then all the verbalizations and interpretations whereby this body communicates to the world around it are simply explications of the fact of its presence.

—*The Royal Priesthood,* 74–75

THE MANDATE OF THE CHURCH

Praising God is at the very center of the Christian church's mandate. When we gather for worship, when we proclaim the gospel in the world, when we practice acts of love, we are to proclaim the virtues of the one who called us to the light and who made us into the people of God. At this point we must call special attention to the aspect of this mandate that has to do with our relationship to the state and to evil.

The posture of the Christian in relation to evil fits into the category of "following Jesus." This concept has become so familiar, so commonplace, so cheap, that we do not properly understand what following really means. What it means is something completely revolutionary.

The early church believed that God was at work within the church by means of Jesus Christ living on within it. The apostle Paul could say that it was no longer he himself who lived;

rather Christ was living in him. He could claim that he could do all things through Christ (Phil. 4:13); he could go even further and claim that in his own flesh he was filling up what was still missing in the suffering of Christ (Col. 1:24). For us these claims, especially the last one, seem strange. To dare to make such audacious claims about one's own faith journey offends our pious sensibilities; it seems repugnant to our modesty, to the humility with which we are accustomed to speaking of faith issues. We would consider it presumptuous if persons were to talk about themselves in this way today, as if that person's life was in some special way bound up with Christ himself.

Yet it is precisely in this seeming presumptuousness that the heart of the Christian faith lies. The early Christians had the audacity to believe quite literally in the Holy Spirit. If it seems too presumptuous to us, if it does not seem humble enough, when Paul speaks without any embarrassment of Christ's work in him, then we should ask ourselves if our humility has not stolen our courage to believe in the Holy Spirit today.

If the church believed such things about itself and testified to their reality, then the church did not view the way of the cross that the church traveled in following Jesus (Mark 10:39; Luke 14:26ff.; John 15:20) as some sort of extra moral achievement, something which would have been optional and commendable, but which they could have done without. They viewed it as something that belongs to the very essence of God's salvation plan for the world. The cross-carrying following which the church practices, which is the continuing life of Jesus through his Spirit in the members of his body, is not an implication, something tacked on; rather, it is part of his saving work. That is what the New Testament means when it speaks of following, of the body of Christ, of the Holy Spirit — that God's continuing work today is no less valid, no less divine, no less urgent than it was from the start. Just as God was at work through the person of God's own Son, so God continues to be at work in the church in the form of the Spirit.

— *Discipleship as Political Responsibility,* 21–22

Worship is the communal cultivation of an alternative construction of society and history. That alternative construction
of history is celebrated by telling the stories of Abraham (and
Sarah and Isaac and Ishmael), of Mary and Joseph and Jesus, of
cross and resurrection and Peter and Paul, of Peter of Cheltchitz
and his Brothers, of George Fox and his Friends. How point-
edly, and at what points, this celebrated construction will set
us at odds with our neighbors, will of course depend on the
neighbors.   — *The Priestly Kingdom*, 43

The view that the Christian church and not the state stands in
the middle of God's rule over the world is not only a statement
of faith; it is also historical fact. Schools and hospitals, honesty
and a work ethic are achievements of Christianity; it is not the
state that brought these about. Just as the church of the Middle
Ages developed schools and hospitals, so also Christians today
can and should be pioneers in the carrying out of ministries that
the state, for lack of ideas or interest, is not well-equipped (e.g.,
voluntary services, nonviolent conflict resolution, humane treatment of those with mental illnesses). And if Christians have a
responsibility in terms of general welfare services (which should
not be left to the state alone), this is even more true with respect
to the central mandate of the Christian church, "to proclaim
the virtues of the One who called them into the light." In fact,
in terms of its service to the state and to the general welfare,
the church serves most effectively and in its own most essential
and irreplaceable way when it seriously goes about the business
of being Christian, proclaiming the gospel, modeling an exem-
plary community life, and praying for all people. The Christian
who wants to put the role of Christian living into second place
in order to serve the state as a first priority is like a musician
who leaves the stage in order to work as an usher in the concert
hall. Of course the usher is also necessary; but the musician cannot be replaced in his or her role. And musicians, of all people,
should know that they are of most value when they perform the
role that no one else can fill. If the musician is not on stage,

and there is therefore no concert, then the usher's role has no meaning either.

— *Discipleship as Political Responsibility,* 44–45

THE IMPORTANCE OF DOXOLOGY

The life of the church's character is doxological. *Not only does the Church proclaims God not only as worthy, as sovereign, but also as victor. God is not simply the one who by nature possesses or merits praise:* God is also the one who is, and has always been, in the process of leading us along in the train of Christ's triumphal procession (Col. 1:14–15).

Earlier when discussing the "scandal of particularity," I referred to the "wider wisdom" with which we are tempted to make Jesus' rewards less precarious and his call less threatening. Now I must return to that theme by observing that when this phenomenon relates to social ethics there is a specific body of alternative wisdom marked by the fact that it not only comes from somewhere else than Jesus but also, necessarily, tells us to do something other than what Jesus tells his disciples to do. Jesus tells us to love our enemies, including holding their lives sacred. The orders of creation, known through the specific locations of some of us in civil responsibility, tell us that for the sake of our love for the life of some nearer neighbor we might need to destroy the enemy neighbor. Jesus tells us to share our bread and our money: those of us who have the particular calling of entrepreneur or of banker should do just the opposite, because there is a structure in the order of things that declares certain spheres to be independent of the pertinence of those instructions from Jesus. One would hardly admit that those other values have the status of idols, since it is claimed that God, as the creator who set things up before Jesus, or the Spirit who keeps on leading since then, has provided them. Still the effect is to relativize the theme that Christ is victor. Partly it says that "victory" is not yet accomplished since we still need to haggle with "realism" to determine how much obedience we can get away with.

We must thus deny any claim to glory or authority made on behalf of alternative value definitions, even if they be affirmed as complementary to God's will or part of it. When I say doxology, that means not only that the glory of God is verbally recognized but that it is celebrated. The word points not simply to an awareness or a conviction but to a spirituality and the cultivation of a distinctive consciousness. To celebrate, and to celebrate repeatedly in memory of Jesus, the glory of God as righteous and as sovereign means to cultivate explicitly an alternative consciousness, to maintain a sense of reality running against the stream of the unquestioningly accepted commonplaces of the age....

That is my first point, and an obvious one: ethics, in the technical sense of our discipline, which analyzes the conditions of validation of dispositions, decisions, and actions, is not an autonomous discipline. It always is and always properly should be in the service of some cosmic commitment or other. There is no nonsectarian "scratch" to start from, beneath or beyond particular identities, no neutral common ground that some sort of search for "foundations" could lay bare. To disengage the structure of the subjacent cosmology must therefore be prior to describing the conceptual mechanics of the moral discourse itself.

There is therefore no one right place for ethics "as such" to begin. It is insufficient to own that ethics is a subdiscipline of ecclesiology or of anthropology or of social science (as it is academically). More important is that all of the intellectual disciplines of critical articulation and reconstruction are embedded in a larger life process. The choir in the heavenly vision sings that that "larger process" is praise, and that it rules the world....

To see history doxologically is to be empowered and obligated to discern, down through the centuries, which historical developments can be welcomed as progress in the light of the Rule of the Lamb and which as setbacks. Not all historical movement is forward. Thus to "discern the signs of the times" is not the same as ascribing to God the course of events as such. Such ascription would be fatalism. That does need to be said, since both socialist and capitalist schemes of progress, to say nothing of the wilder fascist and nationalist claims, do pretend to be able to read a moral lesson off of the surface of history as such. Nor does it mean that we should welcome specific political victories as providential signals, as did Eusebius in heralding Constantine's power as the beginning of the millennium. That would be triumphalism, even if the victors can for the moment convince themselves that (for them) it is liberation. Nor can it be the same as simply defending the biological and anthropological givenness of a society as it stands, which some have called the order of nature or of creation. That would be patriarchalism. In most historical cases it has meant one form or another of *apartheid*.

For there to be accountable discernment of the meaning of particular events within history there must be criteria, themselves part of history yet discernible within it, whereby to discriminate between the setbacks and the steps forward. To that end we have to know, and we do know, as did John's readers, that the slain Lamb before the throne in the heavenly hall was not just one more personage tacked onto the libretto of the vision of Isaiah, but stood for Jesus the crucified Jew. His mother, bearing the name of the songstress of the battle of the Reed Sea, Moses' sister, gave him the name of Moses' successor, as the angel said she should, because he would liberate his people. He was crucified because although his very presence threatened the bearers of power, he waged his holy war nonviolently. He was crucified because as herald of the messianic age he articulated the fulfilling of the law in such a way that love of neighbor is transmuted into love of enemy. The image of a slaughtered Lamb is no empty cipher; it is the code reference, utterly transparent to John's addressees, to the simple narrative substance of the work and the words — not the words without the work nor the work without the words — of that particular Palestinian populist, in all of his Jewishness and all of his patience....

To discern our moral setting doxologically is to learn to derive behavior from good news, not from the concern for justification. Scripture scholars have been seeing and saying for some time that the so-called "beatitudes," or *makarisms*, in the Sermon on the Mount are not statements of impossible moral rigorism but of gospel. When Jesus says, "*makarioi*, blessed are they who...,*" that adjective does not mean "virtuous" or "meritorious"; it means, rather, "fortunate, well-off, privileged." In colloquial American: "good for them!" The ascription of blessedness is inseparable from the proclamation of the kingdom's imminence. Some people are meek: "good for them!" for the kingdom is breaking in, and the earth is their legacy. Some people hunger for justice: "good for them!" for the kingdom is on the way, and they shall be sated. That action is right which fits the shape of the kingdom to come. Moral validation is derived from the imminent kingdom that Jesus announces, not from the righteous state of affairs our action promises to bring about. Moral being and behaving are primordially proclamation or celebration. Only derivatively are they debatable positions in value theory or efficacy. That is why the prologue to the Sermon ends by saying that people watching the kingdom-like behavior of Jesus' hearers will "give the praise to your Father in heaven." ...

To see history doxologically is to own the Lamb's victory in one's own time. Martin Luther King Jr. is one of the victims who in our century have enabled us to keep talking about the power of meekness. The power of his vulnerability taught us again something about the weakness of Caesar. The provisions of the United States Constitution and its amendments and the solemn oaths of office of generations of white officeholders had been powerless, for ninety years after emancipation, to keep the promise of letting blacks into the civil community. It took the principled noncooperation of America's black minority to enable elite powerbearers, whether the shrewd pragmatist Johnson or the more programmatic Kennedys before him, to make small steps toward being honest with the American dream. It took the churches of the underdogs to move the churches and the synagogues of the comfortable — and then only some of them — to support the most modest steps toward the most elementary public morality in matters of race.

Tolstoy was right: progress in history is borne by the underdogs. It was not the strong but the weak, not the persons exercising the responsible power of office but those excluded, who could and did take decisive steps to save America's face and to enable such movement forward, as we have seen.
— *The Royal Priesthood*, 123, 129, 132–33, 136, 137

My point in putting doxology before ethics was that too often our cultural ethics, especially social ethics, is reduced to a form of engineering: how to do what you have to with the least pain. We calculate costs and benefits on the basis of a deterministic understanding of how history goes. Then the place of piety is to help us live with the inevitable pain. If you are more Wesleyan, your warmed heart will make you try harder. If you are more Calvinist, your confidence in predestination will make you try harder. If you are Lutheran, your trust in God's forgiving you will make you stop trying so hard, but by the paradox of grace that will make you do just as well. For all of the above, dogma and spirituality contribute to the setting of the mood of ethics, but not to its substance.

For our apostolic predecessors, the form of the life of faith in society was not in that sense derivative. They did not have in one corner of their casuistry a place to discuss the pros and cons of killing in extreme circumstances. They were living in and into a new world, one in which that corner had no place.
— *The War of the Lamb*, 40

WHY THE CHURCH NEEDS THEOLOGIANS

One reason the faithful church must have theologians is that all the other churches do. The function of theology is to be

suspicious of theology. We might like to short-circuit that suspi-
cion by claiming to have no theology, but that is of course not
a possible solution. The anti-intellectuals and antitheological
people have a theology too. They are just not careful about it.
Liberals who want to accept all positions also have a theology.
The one kind of theology they reject is the one that draws lines
like Jesus did. It is interesting that the people who today claim
it is now hard to talk about these things are very much on a
theological wavelength, especially if they say, "God is dead."
That position has a massive dogmatic concern. It always talks
about proper language, whether the word "God" means anything, what you mean by *kenosis,* and what you can say if you
cannot talk about ethics. If you do not find meaning anymore
in the word "God," they say, at least you can find meaning in
what a good person Jesus was. But you do not find in the God-
is-dead literature what it means to be a good person, whether
being like Jesus means that you are nonresistant, or what to
do about sex if you want to be faithful. They still talk about
the doctrinal, dogmatic, and linguistic concerns as such, rather
than finding discipleship a key to the linguistic concern. So the
antitheological trends are not antitheological. They are theological but anticritical. They are against being careful, against
moral bindingness as a form, against a covenant community as
the context of ethics and theology, against servanthood as the
substance of ethics and of theology. So, against antitheological
trends, when 2 Timothy 1:13–14 tells you to pay attention to
the words you were given and not to dispute about words, it
is a good description of what needs to be done and not just a
paradox.   *— Preface to Theology,* 395

The New Testament records indicate the presence in the early
communities of a particular functionary known as the teacher
(*didaskalos*). Which of the these functions are we to think of
this person as exercising: a catechetical one or a corrective one?
Perhaps there was still something else which was done under
that heading. The teacher's function is unique among those to
which we find reference in the apostolic writings in the fact

that it is specifically described in the epistle of James as a risky function that not many should seek to discharge. This is quite different from the general Pauline pattern that encourages everybody to seek all the gifts (1 Cor. 14:5: all speak in tongues, all prophesy; 1 Tim. 3:1: it is fine to want to be a bishop).

The reason for this caution, we are told, is that the tongue is "an unruly member." Our subjective individualism makes us think of "tongue" as the individual's capacity for speech and of the "unruliness" then as a tendency to speak impulsively, unkindly, or carelessly. One must doubt whether James was so modern. The "tongue" in any Aryan language means the language, the phenomenon of language, and the social reality of communication. Language is unruly in that playing around with words or trying to be consistent in our use of words or dealing with issues by defining terms is a constant source of contestation and confusion. Here is James' caution.

So it is too that Timothy can at the same time be invited to "follow the pattern of the sound words" which he had received from Paul (2 Tim. 1:13) and be warned against "disputing about words, which does no good, but only ruins the hearers" (2 Tim. 2:14). The teacher is then someone charged with care about verbal formulations, who must serve in the awareness that such instruments of the faith are at the same time both indispensable and misleading. It is with language as it is with the rudder of a ship, the bit in the horse's mouth, or the flame igniting a forest: there is a multiplication effect whereby any mistake in balance or aim produces greater damage through the leverage of language.

What does this have to do with how the Bible functions in theology? First of all, the apostle warns that the Bible itself is the victim of that flexibility and leverage. Canonical scripture used by communities to shape their identity has that characteristic of being subject to manipulation in order to support whatever the later interpreters of the tradition want to have ratified. There is a sense in which the objectivity of the scriptural text in its unchanging wording can be appealed to as a corrective against the most highly fanciful flights of redefinition, but it would be part of the naivete against which the apostle warns us if we were to take that objectivity as a guarantee. It is rather the risk of abuse to which canonical texts are subject that calls on the teacher to be more restrained than the poets and prophets in the interpretations that he or she allows people to commend toward one another. The wording of the Bible is not an empowering ratification giving the theologian a special advantage in the knowledge of truths qualitatively different from the truths other people can know. The Bible is, rather, the victim of the corrosive and distorting effect of the leverage of language, and the theologian is its defender.

Everyone ought to read the Bible, and all ought to be free to interpret it soberly in relevance to their own situations. What we need the *didaskalos* for is to defend the historical objectivity of what the text said in the first place against the leverage of overly confident or "relevant" applications. Already in the early church this was a task that called for linguistic sophistication. One needed to know how discerningly to control the tongue. Today it is far clearer how such discernment can and must use the tools of linguistic science. The ancient concept of a "simple sense" of scripture to be played off against the "fuller sense" and the allegorical sense of the text is obviously oversimple, but the concern that it represented is still appropriate. There are forms of articulation which are fruitlessly speculative, destructively relativizing, or unwholesomely accommodating. The task of the *didaskalos* is to defend the difference between the organic fidelity of our interpretation now and the meaning of the message then, as well as to oppose other "adaptations" or "applications" that constitute betrayal.

The fact that people are tempted to abuse scripture by calling on *it* to support whatever they believe is one of the reasons it is inappropriate most of the time to think that the primary theological debate is about whether the biblical text is authoritative or not. Too many people are affirming its authority by claiming its support for interpretations that a more adequate hermeneutic will reject. The theologians' task is more often to defend the text against a wrong claim to its authority than to affirm in some timeless and case-free way that it has authority.

— *To Hear the Word,* 75–77

QUESTIONING THE "GOSPEL OF REVOLUTION"

The difference between this New Testament ethic and that of our age is most clearly demonstrated by what Jesus says about serving and ruling. " 'The kings of the Gentiles lord it over them; and those in authority over them are called benefactors. But not so with you...' " (Luke 22:25–26; cf. Matt. 20:25). In modern parlance, "public service" has become the standard euphemism for the exercise of power, thus fulfilling in the name of the "Christian calling" what Jesus ironically said about pagan rulers, namely, that they glorify the exercise of power over people as being "benefaction." Now Jesus and the New Testament writers following him do not reject rulership because the world is coming to an early end, nor because it is ethically impure (when measured, as Reinhold Niebuhr would measure it, by the standards of absolute selflessness), nor because the people who exercise it are always evil brutes. They do not say that the world can get along without such powers; but neither do they suggest that if by conquest or by elections we put Christians in all those positions they would do a much better job. They simply say that it was the mission of the Son of Man to serve and not to rule and that his disciples will follow him in the same path. If there is to be any solid critique of the contemporary wave of enthusiasm for religiously glorified revolution, it must not be in the name of religiously glorified conservatism nor of social unconcern or neutrality or withdrawal but rather an expression of an ethic of social involvement as servants derived from the person Jesus, whose messianity and lordship we affirm and of whom we confess (whether the "action" to this effect be visible or not) that his way of servanthood shall triumph.

Thus what is questionable about the "gospel of revolution" as currently being propagated by the popularizers is not that it is too revolutionary but rather that it is just a new edition of the same old pattern of seeking in the name of God to make history come out right instead of seeking in the train of Christ only to be servant.   — *The Royal Priesthood, 95*

RETHINKING THE WAY WE READ
THE HISTORY OF CHRISTIANITY

The first mistake Christians have tended to make — for the last thousand years when thinking about Jews — is to forget the "Jewishness" of Christianity, in such a way that we take for granted that the relationship between the two faiths, the two streams of history, could begin with their separateness.

I contend that the valid reading of the history of Jews and Christians must begin with one movement. We can best begin our open search for new light on the Jewish-Christian schism of the second and third centuries (not really of the first) by clarifying an indispensable corrective emphasis concerning historical method. That is the historian's axiom: *It did not have to be.*

There is no error more natural, and perhaps there are few errors more damaging in the reading of history, than the assumption that events had to go the way they did. When the historian tries to "make sense" of an event, it is natural that the effort should proceed by way of understandings of causation. We seek to enlarge our grasp of all the factors that were present in the situation. The more carefully we look, the more naturally we see how those factors that we have found to be important pointed in the direction of what finally happened. We feel we have adequately explained an event when we have constructed a line of "causation" such that we can now see that it could hardly have gone otherwise.

As natural as that explanatory task is for the historian, it does a fundamental disservice to real understanding of what

was going on *then*. For the people in the period we are talking about — whatever period, who knew much more than we
do about all of those facts, did not at all know that things were
going to have to go a certain way. Some of them were quite
conscious that they were making decisions, sometimes agoniz-
ing decisions, about which way things would go. Others felt
powerless in the face of forces pushing them in the wrong direction. Some feared or hoped or prayed about the outcomes, later
finding that some of the fears and some of the hopes were actu-
alized. At other points, they were surprised by outcomes which
they would not have expected or even considered.

We therefore do violence to the lived reality of history as it
really was if in our concern to make sense of it after the fact
we let our explanatory schemes rob its actors of the integrity of
their indecision as well as of their decision-making.

For simplicity's sake, I state this with regard to specific event-
decisions that we can talk about as if they were made at
identifiable points in time. The same is even more true if we
can seek to narrate the kind of decisive developments which,
although utterly conclusive once they have reached an end
point, took years or even generations to "happen." Our particular theme, the Jewish-Christian schism, was this kind of
development. There was never a single event by that name.
After it had conclusively taken place, it seemed to everyone to
be utterly natural that it should have come to pass. Yet there
was a space of at least fifty years — twice that in most respects,
during which it had not happened, was not inevitable or clearly
predictable — and was not chosen by everyone, not even by
everyone who finally was going to have to accept it.

We do violence to the depth and density of the story if,
knowing with the wisdom of later centuries that it came out
as it did, we box the actors of the first century into our wisdom about their children's fate in the second. We thereby refuse
to honor the dignity and the drama of their struggle, and the
open-endedness of their questioning and the variety of paths
available to them until one answer, not necessarily the best one,
not necessarily one anyone wanted, was imposed on them....

Neither Jesus, nor Paul, nor the apostolic communities rejected normative Judaism. This is true first of all, of course, on the superficial level, with all the semantic clarity of tautology. If there was no such thing as normative Judaism no one could have univocally rejected it or been rejected by it. But the point is far more fundamental. What Jesus himself proposed to his listeners was nothing other than what he claimed as the normative vision for a restored and clarified Judaism, namely, the proper interpretation of the Jewish scriptures and tradition for this present, in the light of the New Age that he heralded. Jesus rejected certain other teachings, and he scolded certain other people, as did all Jewish teachers, but he never granted that the traditions and the people he was challenging or reprimanding were qualified interpreters of Torah. He claimed that he himself represented that, and that those other teachers were misled and misleading in their contrary efforts to interpret the tradition.

There is in the gospel accounts of the ministry of Jesus nowhere a rejection of Judaism as a stream of history or a group of people. With regard specifically to the law (Torah), Jesus' attitudes are all affirmative. He said he had come not to destroy the law — or even relax it — but rather to *fulfill* it. He claimed to defend its intent against interpretations that would destroy its meaning or dull its edge. He appealed both to the historical experience of Jews and to their canonical writings to authenticate and illuminate everything he taught. He placed himself completely within that history, with no reference to other histories or sources of wisdom like those from which syncretists or a Jewish philosopher like Philo would borrow.

At points where Jesus entered into debate, it was a debate about the proper meaning of the Jewish scriptures and traditions, never an effort to relativize or deny that heritage. Within the debate on the meaning of the tradition, which is part of the ongoing identity of any living human community, his preference was for return to the "original" or the "radical" meaning of teachings on the sovereignty of God and the imperative of obedience. Sometimes in dialogue Jesus reached back to what he claimed Moses really meant. In one case (Matt. 19, about divorce) he reached back beyond a concession "Moses" had made to human frailty, to restore the original intent of creation, but he always did this within an absolutely Jewish context and in Jewish terms. The freedom he claimed to redefine was *no greater* than the freedom taken by the earlier prophets and canonical writers as they each in their time had also reworked living traditions, or than the freedom taken by later rabbis.

Similarly, the apostle Saul/Paul never surrendered his claim that a true child of Abraham must share the faith in the son of the promise made to Abraham. Those Israelites who had not yet seen Jesus the Promised One were not thereby for Paul mainline Jews, or authentic Jews, but rather Jews not yet accepting the fulfillment of the promises made to their father. In all of his polemic against people who were making what he considered to be a wrong use of the values of the Hebrew heritage (the law, the ritual, circumcision, *kashrut*), Paul never suggested that his adversaries were typical Jews, or that the values they were using wrongly were unimportant, or that he wanted his own disciples to be anything other than good Jews.

— *The Jewish-Christian Schism Revisited,* 43–44, 49–50

THE PROBLEM WITH PROGRESS

The first thing we must do is ask the basic question: Was it progress when the Roman state became Christian in the fourth century? Most church historians and theologians have viewed it as that, starting with Constantine's contemporary Eusebius and continuing on through the Reformation and for many on up to the present. Lying behind all the changes that have occurred is this one, the first and most important of them all. The way we evaluate this change will not only determine our stance in relation to the state, but also our concept of the church itself. That this change was very important is of course a claim with which we agree. But the question is: Was it a change for the better, a change that we evaluate positively in our Christian thinking? The Middle Ages and the Reformation claimed that it was.

The first thing to be clear about is that the New Testament contains no expectation of such "progress"; that is, there is no expectation in the New Testament that there would be a basic change, one to be evaluated positively, in the relationship between the church and the world. Of course the state can change its stance on things; the state can follow through on its mandate (Rom. 13) or it can make itself into a false god (Rev. 13); but whichever it does it is still pagan. The New Testament does not reveal an expectation that things will improve. On the contrary, it expects the situation will worsen for the church, resulting in even more serious persecution and many Christians falling from the faith. If we evaluate the "Christianizing of the state" in light of the New Testament's own terms and value judgments, then we should be thinking of the change as "falling away" rather than as "progress."

The birth hour for the Anabaptist movement struck in Zurich in October 1523, when the reformer Ulrich Zwingli handed over the question of whether or not to dispense with the unbiblical practice of the mass to the city council in Zurich. Zwingli could do that only because he, along with the other reformers and with the Middle Ages, believed that those in the city council were not only Christians, but were Christians worthy of special honor who were specially led by God. This is where Simon Stumpf and Conrad Grebel cried out, "Stop!" In their view, the scriptures alone remain the authority, even for the external life of the church, even if the state calls itself Christian. If the Mass is unbiblical, then government officials, even if they are Christians, *especially* if they are Christians, have no right to retain it. At this point, and not at the time of their first baptism, the Anabaptist movement became a concrete historical reality. The right to exist for the Anabaptists did not come about because of their baptismal practices, nor because of the social ethic they adopted, nor because they refused to bear arms or take oaths. The right to exist for the Anabaptists emerged from their basic refusal to accept any authority, even if it claims to be Christian, alongside or above the Bible. The Anabaptists responded with a clear "No" to the idea that the situation can change so much that the New Testament is no longer a valid authority, and to the idea that the state can in fact be Christian. If they were wrong in these basic convictions, then Anabaptism (and also Mennonitism) has no valid reason to exist; after all, every other issue, whether their convictions about baptism, their understanding of church, discipleship, or social ethics, or their preference for tolerance, is related to their posture towards scripture. —*Discipleship as Political Responsibility,* 35–37

THE TRUTH OF
THE DIASPORA SITUATION

It is true that many Western Christians of all confessions have conceded as a fact that the axioms of Christendom no longer obtain, or that Christians are now in a "Diaspora situation." Yet to make this concession in the face of Enlightenment and political pluralism is far less than to appropriate it theologically and still less than having had the theological tools to denounce the error of establishment when it was dominant. Being willing to relinquish power when one has lost it anyway and to affirm the rights of dissent after the United Nations has done so is mature and sober but not as prophetic as it would have been to call for religious liberty and disestablishment when they were not in style. If then we wish to test the theological claims of an alternative global perspective, it is fitting to distinguish between those traditions that disavowed Constantine and the others who can adjust to his passing.

But the deepest need for making the disavowal explicit lies outside the Christian interconfessional debate. There are in the Middle East hosts of Arabs for whom Christianity is still most deeply understood through the memory of the Crusades. There are Jews here whose fundamental memory of Christianity is the pogrom or the Holocaust. Others of longer memory think back to Spain where an "act of faith" used to mean an execution. We do not disavow Constantine because we enjoy concern with

either our guilt or our innocence, and still less out of denominational self-righteousness, but because all that we ultimately have
to contribute in interfaith dialogue is our capacity to get out of
the way so that instead of, or beyond, us or our ancestors, us
or our language systems, us or our strengths or weaknesses, the
people we converse with might see Jesus.

It is that simple: but that is not simple. It will not happen
without repentance. If we mean the Jesus of history, the Jewish
Jesus of the New Testament, then even here in the land of his
birth — to say nothing of Benares or Peking or Timbuctoo —
there is no alternative but painstakingly, feebly, repentantly,
patiently, locally, to disentangle that Jesus from the Christ of
Byzantium and of Torquemada. The disavowal of Constantine
is then not a distraction but the condition of the historical
seriousness of the confession that it is Jesus Christ who is Lord.
                                        — *The Royal Priesthood*, 260–61

WHY THE OTHERNESS OF
JERUSALEM MATTERS

God's choosing to pitch his tent in our midst is his mercy, not
our merit or our property. That God chooses neutral ground (or
foreign ground) as the way to be graciously in our midst points
to a truth, which all three Abrahamic faiths have retained,
though in different ways. God is never our God in the sense
of our possessing him. God's compassionate intentions always
include the others, the outsiders, the nations, the sojourners.
The fact that Jerusalem is spoken of by apostles and prophets
as "beyond," or as "to come," as "above" or "holy" or "heavenly," reflects the self-limiting modesty that that transcendence
demands of the believer. It would be wrong to philosophize
any of these "otherness" terms, i.e., to explain the otherness in
terms of some metaphysical dualism. Suffice it that they all relativize the empirical, manipulable "reality." They relativize the
given in favor of the gift.

The same self-limiting understanding takes other forms in the later history. In the Jewish experience it is represented by Jeremiah's acceptance of *galut* (exile) as mission and by the much later development of the theory of the Noachic covenant, whose observance by the Gentiles may entitle them to share in the age to come. In the Christian experience it is the place of mission to the Gentiles as mark of the messianic age.

That the otherness of Jerusalem, as cipher for the otherness of God, points us away from possessiveness and toward the redefinition of providence so as to favor the outsider, is an easily forgotten truth. We all fall back easily into provincial self-definitions that reduce the Most High God to a graven image by reducing his causes to our own. Christians have done that the most culpably, especially since their alliance with Imperial Rome, but the other faith families enjoy no automatic exemption from the same temptation, and terrestrial Jerusalem has been one of the victims of their conflicts ever since.

— *The Jewish-Christian Schism Revisited,* 161–62

3

A Cosmic Vision

Confident that Jesus is Lord and that his lordship is exercised in history through the church, Yoder is then free to suggest how this same lordship is exercised over the rest of the world. Building on what has been intimated in the previous section, this third series begins with four readings that flesh out the relationship between the church and the powers that rule the world, readings that to argue that the appropriate division of reality is not between the sacred and the profane, not between the spiritual and the physical, and not between the ecclesiastical and the civil. Rather, these readings reveal that Yoder's account of reality is divided between those who confess Christ as Lord and those who do not. In this way, he envisions the church always existing "in the midst of things," by which he means that the church always exists firmly within the world. Within the world and in a truly nonsectarian fashion, the church rejects those things that contradict the lordship of Christ and affirms those things that complement it.

In an attempt to exemplify how the church performs this discerning task, the next three readings describe various examples that Yoder provides of the church's affirmation of complementarity: the first example is the affirmation of Tolstoy's insight that "the cure for evil is suffering"; the second is an embrace of the heart of the spiritual vision shared by both Gandhi and

King; the third is the elevation of the acts of faithfulness per-
formed by a wide range of "witnesses," from César Chávez to
Shantidas (Lanza del Vasto) to Danilo Dolci to Dom Helder
Câmara.

In conclusion, the final two readings provide contextualizing
observations that acknowledge the current state of the world
and the world as it will be. Having grasped how Yoder understands the relationship between the church and the world in
this way, one is finally prepared to grapple with his description
of the practices and practical considerations of the church, the
subject of the next series of readings.

GOD'S DOMINION AND
THE POWERS OF THE WORLD

From the very earliest record of the witness and worship of
the church in the first chapters of the book of Acts to the lat-
est portions of the New Testament canon, the affirmation is
unchanging that Jesus Christ, ascended to the right hand of
God, is now exercising dominion over the world. The passage
from Psalm 110 is the one section of the Old Testament most
frequently cited or alluded to in the New Testament.

In order to grasp what Old and New Testaments mean
by this kind of statement, we need first to understand how
the Bible sees human affairs to be dominated by superhu-
man powers, referred to biblically under many names (thrones,
principalities, powers, archangels, dominions), which are often
grouped by interpreters under some such heading as *angelic* or
demonic. These powers are seen as invisibly determining human
events; in biblical language powers would be roughly the equivalent of the modern term "structures," by which psychological
or sociological analysts refer to the dimensions of cohesiveness
and purposefulness which hold together human affairs beyond
the strictly personal level, especially in such realms as that of
the state or certain areas of culture. In short, the powers govern

that realm which the Bible refers to as the *world* (*kosmos* in the Johannine writings, *aion houtos* according to Paul).

The triumphant affirmation of the New Testament is that Jesus Christ by his cross, resurrection, ascension, and the pouring out of his Spirit has triumphed over the powers. This is the concrete meaning of the term "Lord." The significance of the present period of history, from Pentecost to the parousia, is that "he must reign until he has put all his enemies under his feet" (1 Cor. 15:25)....

Jesus made it clear that the nationalized hope of Israel had been a misunderstanding and that God's true purpose was the creation of a new society, unidentifiable with any of the local, national, or ethnic solidarities of any time. This new body, the church, as aftertaste of God's loving triumph on the cross and foretaste of his ultimate loving triumph in his kingdom, has a task within history. History is the framework in which the church evangelizes, so that the true meaning of history is the fact that God has chosen to use it for such a "scaffolding" service....

In spite of the present visible dominion of the "powers" of "this present evil age," the triumph of Christ has already guaranteed that the ultimate meaning of history will not be found in the course of earthly empires or the development of proud cultures, but in the calling together of the "chosen race, royal priesthood, holy nation," which is the church of Christ. The church is not fundamentally a source of moral stimulus to encourage the development of a better society, though a faithful church should also have this effect, it is for the sake of the church's own work that society continues to function. The meaning of history — and therefore the significance of the state — lies in the creation and the work of the church. The reason for Christian prayer in favor of the political authorities is that "God our Savior desires all men to be saved and to come to the knowledge of the truth" (1 Tim. 2). The function of the state in maintaining an ordered society is thereby a part of the divine plan for the evangelization of the world.

— *The Christian Witness to the State*, 8–11, 13

DUALITY AND THE DUTY
OF THE CHURCH

So it is right that we should begin at this point. The definition of the gathering of Christians is their confessing Jesus Christ as Lord. The definition of the whole of human society is the absence of that confession, whether through conscious negation or simple ignorance, despite the fact that Christ is ("objectively," "cosmically") Lord for them as well. The duality of church and world is not a slice separating the religious from the profane, nor the ecclesiastical from the civil, nor the spiritual from the material. It is the divide on this side of which there are those who confess Jesus as Lord, who in so doing are both secular and profane, both spiritual and physical, both ecclesiastical and civil, both individual and organized, in their relationships to one another and to others. The difference as to whether Christ is confessed as Lord is a difference on the level of real history and personal choices, not a difference of realm or levels or even dimensions.

This is not the dualist slice between two "planes of reality," which has been so effectively and properly denounced by Gustavo Gutiérrez as the philosophical defense of political conservatism in the name of the church. It is not the dualism between religious and secular vocations or between ordination and laity, or between Reformed and Anabaptist. Pardon my burdening you with such a long list of ready-to-hand dualisms that are not intended; I have seen too often how their habitual unchallenged use has kept gospel social ethics from being understood....

To say that the first service of the church to the world is to be that part of the world that is already entered upon its fulfillment may seem like withdrawal from concern or involvement beyond the church's membership. This conclusion has been drawn far too often, but when it has been drawn it has not been on the basis of this theological understanding. The sense in which this calling to be first of all the believing community is primary is not a chronological sequence whereby one task must be achieved before there is leisure to turn to the other. The church's being the church is primordial rather in the sense of orientation. In order to be whatever I want to be with all of my time wherever I am I must first be who I am in myself. The priority of authentic identity does not postpone for some later time its implications for worldly living but produces them immediately. We speak of a priority or primordiality in terms of identity and not of sequence.

It is thus a caricature and not what we are talking about when the response is made, "We should be working at righteousness in the world rather than trying first of all to tidy up the purity of the church." The Christian is always engaged in both. The questions that matter are not which to be engaged in, or which to do first, but how each of them is defined and how the definitions of both are related to each other. For those who wish to assert the primordiality or autonomy of the duties of implementing justice in the world, what we need to question is not their stating that those duties are duties but their assumption, hidden behind the caricature quoted above, that the way to do it is to be guided by standards of justice other than those of the incarnation. —*The Royal Priesthood*, 108–9, 119

The believing body is the image that the new world — which in the light of the ascension and Pentecost is on the way — casts ahead of itself. The believing body of Christ is the world on the way to its renewal; the church is the part of the world that confesses the renewal to which all the world is called. The believing body is the instrument of that renewal of the world, to the (very modest) extent to which its message is faithful. It may be "instrument" as proclaimer, or as pilot project, or as pedestal.

For the people of God to be over against the world at those points where "the world" is defined by its rebellion against God, and for us to be in, with, and for the world, as anticipation of the shape of redemption are not alternative strategies. We are not free to choose between them, depending on whether

our tastes are more "catholic" or more "baptist," or depending on whether we think the times are friendly just now or not.
Each dimension of our stance is the prerequisite for the validity
of the other. A church that is not "against the world" in fundamental ways has nothing worth saying to and for the world.
Conversion and separation are not the way to become other-
worldly; they are the only way to be present, relevantly and
redemptively, in the midst of things.   —*Body Politics*, 78

The church precedes the world epistemologically. We know
more fully from Jesus Christ and in the context of the confessed
faith than we know in other ways. The meaning and validity
and limits of concepts like "nature" or of "science" are best
seen not when looked at alone but in light of the confession of
the lordship of Christ. The church precedes the world as well
axiologically, in that the lordship of Christ is the center that
must guide critical value choices, so that we may be called to
subordinate or even to reject those values that contradict Jesus.
    Yet both in the order of knowing and in the order of valu-
ing, the priority of the faith does not exclude or deny everything
else. Insights that are not contradictory to the truth of the Word
incarnate are not denied but affirmed and subsumed within
the confession of Christ. Values that are not counter to his
suffering servanthood are not rejected but are affirmed and
subsumed in his lordship, becoming complementary and instrumental in the exercise of ministry to which he calls his disciples.
This is the point at which H. Richard Niebuhr's notion of
"Christ against culture" misinterprets the minority tradition as
disjunctive rather than integrative.
                                —*The Priestly Kingdom*, 11

OVERCOMING THE POWERS
OF THIS WORLD

If our lostness consists in our subjection to the rebellious
powers of a fallen world, what then is the meaning of the

work of Christ? Subordination to these powers is what makes us human, for if they did not exist there would be no history nor society nor humanity. If then God is going to save his creatures *in their humanity*, the powers cannot simply be destroyed or set aside or ignored. Their sovereignty must be broken. This is what Jesus did, concretely and historically, by living a genuinely and free human existence. This life brought him, as any genuinely human existence will bring anyone, to the cross. In his death the powers — in this case the most worthy, weighty representatives of Jewish religion and Roman politics — acted in collusion. Like everyone, he too was subject (but in his case quite willingly) to these powers. He accepted his own status of submission. But morally he broke their rules by refusing to support them in their self-glorification; and that is why they killed him. Preaching and incorporating a greater righteousness than that of the Pharisees, and a vision of an order of social human relations more universal than the Pax Romana, he permitted the Jews to profane a holy day (refuting thereby their own moral pretensions) and permitted the Romans to deny their vaunted respect for law as they proceeded illegally against him. This they did in order to avoid the threat to their dominion represented by the very fact that he existed in their midst so morally independent of their pretensions. He did not fear even death. Therefore, his cross is a victory, the confirmation that he was free from the rebellious pretensions of the creaturely condition. Differing from Adam, Lucifer, and all the powers, Jesus did "not consider being equal with God as a thing to be seized" (Phil. 2:6). His very obedience unto death is in itself not only the sign but also the first fruits of an authentic restored humanity. Here we have for the first time to do with someone who is not the slave of any power, of any law or custom, community or institution, value or theory. Not even to save his own life will he let himself be made a slave of these powers. This authentic humanity included his free acceptance of death at their hands. Thus it is death that provides his victory: "Wherefore God has exalted him highly, and given him the name which is above very name...that every tongue might confess that Jesus Christ is Lord" (2:9–11)....

If this victory over the powers constitutes the work of Christ, then it must also be a message for the church to proclaim. "To me, less than the least of all the saints," says Paul, "was given the grace to proclaim among the Gentiles the gospel of the inscrutable riches of Christ, and to declare to all what is the dispensation of the mystery hidden since the ages in God, who created all things; so that the manifold wisdom of God should henceforth be made known by means of the church to the principalities and powers in heavenly places, according to the eternal purpose which he set in Jesus Christ our Lord" (Eph. 3:8–11)....

It is thus a fundamental error to conceive of the position of the church in the New Testament in the face of social issues as a "withdrawal" or to see this position as motivated by the Christians' weakness, by their numerical insignificance or low social class, by their fear of persecution, or by scrupulous concern to remain uncontaminated by the world. What can be called the "otherness of the church" is an attitude rooted in strength and not in weakness. It consists in being a herald of liberation and not a community of slaves. It is not a detour or a waiting period, looking forward to better days that one hopes might come a few centuries later; it was rather a victory when the church rejected the temptations of Zealot and Maccabean patriotism and Herodian collaboration. The church accepted as a gift being the "new humanity" created by the cross and not by the sword....

The powers have been defeated not by some kind of cosmic hocus-pocus but by the concreteness of the cross; the impact of the cross upon them is not the working of magical words nor the fulfillment of a legal contract calling for the shedding of innocent blood, but the sovereign presence, within the structures of creaturely orderliness, of Jesus the kingly claimant and of the church, which is itself a structure and a power in society. Thus the historicity of Jesus retains, in the working of the church as it encounters the other power and value structures of its history, the same kind of relevance that the person Jesus had for those whom he served until they killed him.

— *The Politics of Jesus,* 144–45, 147, 148–49, 158

THE SOCIAL FUNCTION OF PAGANS

All evidence to the contrary notwithstanding, the church believed that its Lord was also Lord over the world. The explicit paganism of state, art, economics, and learning did not keep the church from confessing their subordination to him who sits at the right hand of God. This belief in Christ's lordship over the *exousiai* enabled the church, in and in spite of its distinctness from the world, to speak to the world in God's name, not only in evangelism but in ethical judgment as well. The church could take on a prophetic responsibility for civil ethics without baptizing the state or the statesman. The justice the church demanded of the state was not Christian righteousness but human *iustitia;* this it could demand from pagans, not because of any belief in a universal, innate moral sense, but because of its faith in the Lord. Thus the visible distinctness of church and world was not an insouciant irresponsibility; it was a particular, structurally appropriate way, and the most effective way, to be responsible. This attitude was meaningful for the church because it believed that the state was not the ultimately determinative force in history. It ascribed to the state at best a preservative function in the midst of an essentially rebellious world, whereas the true sense of history was to be sought elsewhere, namely, in the work of the church. This high estimation of the church's own vocation explains both its visible distinctness from the world and the demands it addressed to the world. The depth of the church's conviction that its own task was the most necessary enabled it to leave other functions in society to pagans: the church's faith in Christ's lordship enabled it to do so without feeling that it was abandoning them to Satan.

— *The Royal Priesthood,* 56

TOLSTOY AND THE KEY

Tolstoy was first of all a convert, his *Confession,* his *What I Believe,* and his *The Kingdom of God Is Within You* are the interpretations of a profound change of the orientation of a person's life that took place at once from within and from without and made of him a different person than he had been before.

I said that the change came from within. Especially as the story is told in his confession, there was a long period of growing inner awareness of the unworthiness of the life Tolstoy was leading. We might argue that that narration is somewhat fictionalized, made more interesting or more dramatic by painting his earlier life in dark colors or by making the turnabout more sudden and radical than it was. Perhaps his contemplating suicide was not as serious or as sudden as his account makes it. Perhaps there were several small crises rather than one great one. For our purpose, that is unimportant. What is important is the sense in which what led Tolstoy to a change of life direction was intrinsically a part of the distinctive strength that he brought to life: his ability to perceive the depths of human being and relating and to describe that perception dramatically, his great gift of narration and the ability to convince the reader that inside the personages in his stories things really were that way. Thus, when Tolstoy brought this skill at analyzing and portraying to bear on a new set of life questions, there was a quality of strong conviction about his argument. There were a multitude of readers all over the Western world ready to serve as a sounding board. If he had not been the great novelist and reteller of folk tales, he might have had the same experience, but his telling it would not have been heard.

But what we must ask about first is not the hearing but the being. His power of perception and convincing description made it possible for Tolstoy, in his new conviction, to stand or to march against the stream of hostility drawn upon him by his new views. This hostility was elicited not only from the conservative forces of empire and the orthodox ecclesiastical establishment, but also from the critical perspectives of bourgeois Westernization and the advocates of violent revolution. Analyzing and portraying were not simple tricks or skills that were exercised at arm's length, so to speak: they were his mind or his gift. It was in doing so that he was authentic, that he was himself, and that his conviction was irreversible.

The trigger for this change came from outside Tolstoy's own mind. It was not a product of simple organic movement in which what comes later is fully explained on the basis of what was already present. Tolstoy responded to the gospel. What "the gospel" came to mean to him was illuminated by his literary and critical skills but was not the product of those skills. They rather made only more precise and demanding the claims laid on him by a message from another world.

"The gospel" does not mean some vague reference to anything or everything in the Christian message. Within the total Christian tradition — on grounds that he can explain and argue — Tolstoy chooses the scriptures, within the scriptures the New Testament, within them the teachings of Jesus. At the heart of the Christian faith properly understood is not dogma or ritual, but Jesus. At the heart of the meaning of Jesus is his teaching of the kingdom of God. At the heart of that teaching is the Sermon on the Mount. At the heart of the Sermon is the contrast between what had been said by them of old and what "I now say to you." At the core of these antitheses is the love of the enemy and nonresistance to evil.

Every step of that series of concentric reductions is debatable, yet every step as well can be justified on literary and substantial grounds. The result is what Tolstoy calls simply the "key" to the scripture message: the cure for evil is suffering. This key restores the link between the work of Christ and human obedience, which had been forgotten or destroyed through the centuries.

Not only is this one dramatic and scandalous teaching of Jesus internally accredited as the key to the scriptures; it is also the key to what is wrong with the world. It is violence and the hunger for domination that characterize our society and are to blame for the other dimensions of injustice that may be described independently, such as class conflict, economic exploitation, sexual or racial exploitation, etc. The other evils in the world are not adequately explained by virtue of an empty formula like "original sin," nor by means of a materialist reduction such as a dialectic of structural changes that has not yet reached its self-redemption. What is wrong with the world is most fundamentally that people respond to evil with evil and thereby aggravate the spiral of violence.

This centering process is an inclusive rather than an exclusive narrowing. Tolstoy does not exclude any realm of real life, in contrast to the mystic path of negation or the pietistic concentration upon feeling. He rather centers or integrates all of life into one organizing vision. The key opens every room of our previously compartmentalized history.

The key to the good news is that we are freed from prolonging the chain of evil causes engendering evil effects by action and reaction in kind. By refusing to extend the chain of vengeance, we break into the world with good news. This one key opened the door to a restructuring of the entire universe of Christian life and thought. There developed from it a critique of economic exploitation, of military and imperial domination, and of Westernization.   — *Nonviolence,* 19–22

NONVIOLENCE AND
A RELIGIOUS VISION OF HISTORY

Nonviolent action is costly. It includes readiness at least for prison and a degree of risk of loss of life. In some of the experiences of the Gandhian movement, the loss of life was as likely a prospect as it is in a strictly military encounter. Yet the willingness of people to run those risks cannot be rooted in the excitement of adventure or in chauvinistic hatred or the thrill of the risk of a duel, as it is in the military case. Where, then, can it be rooted? It can be rooted only in a religious vision of the congruence between suffering and the purposes of God.

It is not indispensable that their vision of God must be exactly that of Jews or of Christians for such a vision to guide people. Yet it does seem that, for the "faith" of the community active in nonviolence both to sustain and guide the community there must at least be some roughly equivalent conviction that the course of human experience is purposive, that it is borne by the affirmation and not the sacrifice of the dignity of the person, and that redemption is offered to the oppressor and not only to the oppressed. Without those constitutive elements, it will not be possible to keep the defense of the rights of victims from seeking a mere reversal of roles and replacing one oppression with another.

Rooting nonviolence in a religious vision of history forbids that the renunciation of violence be thought of as a mere tactic or technique. That does not exclude the possibility that in given conflict situations there may well be participants who see it only on that level. It was the case in the civil rights struggle in the United States that the leadership of King and his Christian colleagues was accepted by some who did not consider themselves Christian; for others, the renunciation of violence was for the time being a merely "tactical move," which deprived the racist authorities of the pretext for violent retaliation. It was not wrong for either them or King to enter into a tactical alliance in particular situations. Yet it became clear, when the movement came on harder times and their tactical reasons for renouncing violence were no longer promising, that the ways needed to part. It is striking that those in America who from that point forward said that violence would be justified never did actually achieve anything positive by means of violent struggle.

The unity of religious rootage and ethical strategy is not merely intellectual. The planning meetings of the American black struggle were at the same time services of praise and preaching. The marches for freedom were at the same time religious processions, a pattern that was to be established again in another context when Bishop Hélder Câmara of Brazil used the format of the religious procession to gather people in political protest, when their manifestation would not have been otherwise legal.   —*Nonviolence,* 42–43

THE CLOUD OF WITNESSES

Toward the end of the Epistle to the Hebrews (chapter 11), after the author had given an extended description of the acts of faithfulness of Abel and Abraham, and a more brief but still-concrete description of other well-known heroes, the description spreads out or splashes into a list of many other people too numerous to name. In a similar way, in the wake of the major personalities whom we have taken as prototypical (but also to some extent independently of them), there would be others to name if our purpose were doxological like that of the author of Hebrews. There are others whose creativity we would need to describe and whose sacrifices we would chronicle if our purpose were to lift from these stories a series of lessons or generalizations, as the social scientist does. Without providing those details, let it be said that those stories do exist and that their analysis would richly reinforce the lessons described above. The experiences described above are not models to be slavishly imitated. Neither, however, are they rare and odd exceptions (what in current English we call "flukes"); they are prototypes, or (to use a biblical expression) "first fruits." This is corroborated by the later "cloud of witnesses."

To that cloud of witnesses we could add the thousands of American young men who refused their call to military service in the Vietnam War and the wider circle of their friends and sympathizers who gathered in streets and lecture halls to support them. We could add the work of César Chávez, the Mexican-American activist, who enabled farm laborers for the first time to grasp the right to organization and collective bargaining. We could add Lanza del Vasto, or Shantidas, the noble disciple of Gandhi, who brought to the West the *ashram* pattern of devotion, training, and direct action. We could add Danilo Dolci, the Italian poet and architect who first imparted to the victims of Sicily's feudal or bandit culture the courage and organizational vision to defend themselves and prod even the Roman bureaucracy into action. We could watch the work of Archbishop Hélder Câmara, conscience of the conferences of the Roman Catholic bishops of Latin America in their growing courageous readiness to denounce the terrorism of states and counterstates. If the information could flow freely, we could find and congratulate and analyze many others, from other portions of the world, mobilizing other victimized people against other kinds of oppression. It is the global message of that common story which we need now to summarize.

—Nonviolence, 39–40

It is not merely that minority peoples tell stories and majority people don't tell stories, although that is in fact often the case. The believing community has a longer sense of history past and future than do their oppressors, or than majorities unaware of alternatives to their own world. They also see the same facts differently. They do not assume that the only way to read national and political history is from the perspective of the winners. To remember that in every battle there was another side, and sometimes that there were more people on the other side and sometimes more worthy causes, sustains a different understanding of how we want to help history move.

—The Priestly Kingdom, 95

A CONFESSION
CONCERNING THE SYSTEM

The Greek word *cosmos,* which is used here, might best be translated as "the system." It points to the way things fit together: to the networking, the organizing; to the way that God's refractory creation, God's rebellious creatures stick together for evil. Human solidarity is a good thing, but once solidarity has become nationalism, racism, or collective selfishness, it is not. Human rationality is a good thing, but when it has been harnessed to destruction, it is not.

God made his creatures capable of organization through solidarity. When we use those capacities for evil, they still work.

What is wrong with our world is not simply a matter of isolated individual ignorance or isolated evil will. It is not just that
I am a sinner and you another, she a sinner, and they sinners,
and it all adds up. The whole world is worse than the sum of
its parts.

This is a first sobering truth about the task facing the peace
movement. What killed Jesus was a *world*. The men who joined
in executing Jesus were the mere instruments of larger forces.
This is what the apostle Paul meant when he wrote:

> For it is not against human enemies that we have to strug-
> gle, but against the Sovereignties and the Powers who
> originate the darkness in this world. (Eph. 6:12, JB)...

The "challenge of peace" is not, then, just a matter of fixing or
fine-tuning a system of which the other parts are working well.
We are not trying merely to correct one mistake in an otherwise
adequate culture. We are dealing, rather, with an evil that is
representative and prototypical. When you cut across a piece
of wood you find a pattern of lines or circles that we call "the
grain." The grain is not only at the end of the wood; it runs all
the way through the log. You see it at the extremity where the
cutting exposed it.

The arms race is like that. It is the cut that exposes the grain.
The grain is national chauvinism, the assumption of moral superiority inherent in our kind of people and of the right to sacrifice
the security of other people for the sake of our own. The grain
that runs clear through the wood is trust in coercive power to
bend others to our will. If we thought we could do that to our
neighbors with crossbows or with slingshots instead of atomic
weapons, that would be no better morally.

But organization and technology have so multiplied the stakes
that anyone can see the grain. Anyone can see that the evil is
systemic. That is why a particular tactic, such as a nuclear freeze,
even if it is a good political first step, is not enough. It was not
enough in the nineteenth century to stop importing slaves.

One mistake we need to avoid is placing the blame on some
evil people. Most people within "the system" are not nasty.

They do not beat their wives and children. A few of them are brutal, some are selfish or venal, profiteers or racketeers; but most of them are not. They may lack imagination or courage, just as I do.   — *He Came Preaching Peace,* 31–32

THE RELEVANCE OF
TRANSCENDENT HOPE

The relevance of a transcendent hope may sometimes be that of the *spring in the desert.* If, in a desert region, water can be found it is because in some distant and unknown place incalculable quantities of water have sunk into the ground and disappeared. Only because of that infiltration in some distant place, continuing over a long time and developing pressure in a stratum of porous rock, can water be carried under the desert soil. Far away, it can be found as a seemingly miraculous source of sustenance. So it is with deeds of Christian obedience. Lost in the earth, filtering away without being seen or heard, they contribute to the building up of pressure, creating a subterranean reservoir of saving and invigorating power that can be tapped at the point where people are most thirsty. Sociologists may speak of it as the creation of custom, the development of public opinion, or the raising of the general level of capacity for generous conduct. All of these are simply other ways of affirming that the relationship between my obedience and the accomplishment of the purposes of God must include my losing track of my own effectiveness in the great reservoir of the pressure of love....

We are not marching to Zion because we think that by our own momentum we can get there. But that is still where we are going. We are marching to Zion because, when God lets down from heaven the new Jerusalem prepared for us, we want to be the kind of persons and the kind of community that will not feel strange there.   — *The Original Revolution,* 158–59

4

Practices and Practical Considerations

Building on the rich vision sketched in the previous pages, this final section provides various examples of how Yoder's spiritual vision discerns, enables, and motivates appropriate action. The first two readings in this series explore how the nonviolent revelation of God in Jesus calls for our imitation of God's respect for human freedom, even the freedom to choose evil. This conviction is basic to the rest of Yoder's ethics as it is on this basis that violence is ruled out as unchristian.

Of course, Yoder is not so naïve that he misunderstands the radical nature of his vision. Yet he pursues an extrapolation of this nonviolent position in the next nine readings, calmly challenging the temptations facing Christians to find their identity in the nation and to give the application and perceived authority of the just-war position more credence than it deserves. On the other hand, he constructively points toward the ways in which nonviolence has found (and continues to find) its critical voice within the Christian tradition. And, to bring the discussion on war and peace to an end, he reframes the issue in terms of the practice of listening to the leading of the Holy Spirit, who leads one "into all the truth."

The final eight readings are then devoted to displaying the types of virtues and practices that must be cultivated to sustain the community that embodies the rule of Christ. In these pages,

we find the everyday activities of the church — the church that
adopts a minority posture and sides with the oppressed — given
a defining role in a new reality, a new society, the kingdom of
God that is coming and is already here now.

THE RULE OF CHRIST

"When he saw the crowds he went up the hill. There he took his
seat, and when his disciples had gathered round him he began
to address them" (Matt. 5:1–2). When Moses met God on a
mountain and received from him the tables of the law, this law
was for all the children of Israel. When Jesus from another hill
proclaims again the statutes of his rule, it is to his disciples.
This is not a set of moral standards to be imposed on everyone
or on the unconvinced. It is not proposed that persons using
these standards can rule the unbelieving world accordingly, nor
that they will be prosperous and popular. The ethic of discipleship is not guided by the goals it seeks to reach, but by the
Lord it seeks to reflect. It is no more interested in "success" or
in "effectiveness" than he. It is binding only upon those voluntarily enrolled in the band of his followers. It is assumed
that they will be a minority in society; how the world would
look if everyone would behave as they is not a question we
immediately need to answer....

What do I communicate to people about the love of God
by being willing to consider them an enemy? What do I say
about personal responsibility by agreeing to consider them my
enemy when it is only the hazard of birth that causes us to live
under different flags? What do I say about forgiveness if I pun-
ish them for the sins of their rulers? How is it reconcilable with
the gospel — good news — for the last word in my estimate of
any person to be that, in a case of extreme conflict, it could be
my duty to sacrifice that person's life for the sake of my nation,
my security, or the political order that I prefer?

The idea that human life is intrinsically sacred is not a specifically Christian thought. But the gospel itself, the message that

Christ died for his enemies, is *our* reason for being ultimately responsible for the neighbor's — and especially the enemy's — life. We can only say this to the neighbor if we say to ourselves that we cannot dispose of him or her according to our own will. . . .

The first characteristic of the "righteousness of the scribes and Pharisees" is that it makes its standards fulfillable. Loving my neighbor is possible if I may still hate. Keeping rigorously an oath in the name of the Lord God himself is possible if I may still leave room to cheat a little when I swear by Jerusalem or heaven. I can perhaps refrain from killing and from adultery if I may still cherish lustful and hateful thoughts. Thus we still seek to tailor our morals to fit our means, so that we can keep the rules and justify ourselves thereby. The logical circle is vicious. We want to be able to justify ourselves by what we can do so we set our goals within reach. We construct for ourselves a manageable morality that we can handle, without repentance, even if it should not be true that the kingdom of heaven is at hand.

This temptation is still with us, especially with regard to the problems of violence and national egoism, which are our special concern here. One reason most theologies want to replace the Sermon on the Mount with some other standards is just this: they want something possible, something you can teach to all your children and require of all your parishioners, a goal a person can realistically reach. This is a very logical desire, if our goal is to be the moral mentors and "preachers" of a self-justifying civilization, including a service as chaplain to its armies. Jesus' criticism is only that this goal is not the same as being heralds of his kingdom.

The second trait of the "righteousness of the scribes and Pharisees" is that it is external, accessible. We get it out on the surface where we can prescribe and proscribe specific acts as right and wrong. We cannot tell if the heart is pure, but we can identify murder and adultery. We cannot make a man love his wife for life, but we can insist that the divorce proceedings be legal. Legitimacy replaces love as the standard.

Implied in the outwardness and fulfillability is a third characteristic. The righteousness of the scribes and Pharisees assumes
a reasonable degree of legitimate self-interest. It can ask self-
discipline but not self-denial; temperance and moderation, but
not asceticism; it can ask us to bear a yoke, but not a cross.
And so it is today: the limits of moral rigor lie at the point of
survival — national or personal. Do not lie — except to save
your life or country. Do not kill — except killers. Do not save
yourself unless others depend on you. In the Protestant West it
is traditional to accuse Roman Catholic confessional casuistry,
and especially that of the Jesuits, of making too easy accommo-
dations of the moral law to the needs and desires of humans.
But every tradition does this in one way or another....

> But what I tell you is this: Love your enemies and pray
> for your persecutors; only so you can be children of your
> heavenly Father, who makes his sun rise on good and bad
> alike, and sends the rain on the honest and the dishonest.
> If you love only those who love you, what reward can you
> expect? Surely the tax-gatherers do as much as that. And
> if you greet only your brothers, what is there extraordi-
> nary about that? Even the heathen do as much. There must
> be no limit to your goodness, as your heavenly Father's
> goodness knows no bounds. (Matt. 5:44–48)

If everyone had read these verses more carefully, there would
have been less fruitless speculation about whether and in what
sense Christians can and should try to be, or expect to be "perfect." This command does make great problems in theology,
and in the cure of souls, if we take "perfect" to point to a goal
of absolute flawlessness, or of having come to the end of all
possibilities of growth. But Jesus is saying that we should not
love only our friends because God did not love only his friends.
As the parallel statements in verse 45 and in Luke 6 make clear,
we are asked to "resemble God" just at this one point: not in
his omnipotence or his eternity or his impeccability, but simply in the undiscriminating or unconditional character of his
love. This is not a fruit of long growth and maturation; it is

not inconceivable or impossible. We can do it tomorrow if we believe. We can stop loving only the lovable, lending only to the reliable, giving only to the grateful, as soon as we grasp and are grasped by the unconditionality of the benevolence of God. "There must be no limit to your goodness, as your heavenly Father's goodness knows no bounds."

This is one of the keys to the problem of war and legitimate defense. Every argument that would permit the taking of life is in one way or another based on calculations of rights and merits. I prefer the life of those nearest me to that of the foreigner, or the life of the innocent to that of the troublemaker, because my love is conditional, qualified, natural, just like that of everyone else. Jesus does not condemn this normal self-seeking quality — for Gentiles — but he says there is nothing new, nothing special, nothing redemptive or healing about it — "What reward can you expect?" Not only is "perfect love" not limited to those who merit it; it even goes beyond the unjust demands of those who coerce compliance with their will. "Do not resist one who is evil. But if any one strikes you on the right cheek, turn to him the other also" (Matt. 5:39).

This is the origin of the label "nonresistance." The term is stronger and more precise than "nonviolence"; for one can hate, despise, conquer, or crush another without the use of outward violence. But the term is confusing as well. It has been interpreted — by those who reject the idea — to mean a weak acceptance of the intentions of the evil one, resignation to his evil goals. This the text does not call for. The services to be rendered to the one who coerces us — carrying his burden a second mile, giving beyond the coat and the cloak — are to his person, not to his purposes. The "resistance" that we renounce is a response in kind, returning evil for evil. But the alternative is not complicity in his designs. The alternative is creative concern for the person who is bent on evil, coupled with the refusal of his goals.

What in the old covenant was a limit on vengeance — for one eye, only one eye — has now become a special measure of love demanded by concern for the redemption of the offender. This is "perfect love"; this is what it means that not a jot or a tittle will pass from the law until all is filled full....

The most serious hatred is seen not in the act but in the inner attitude toward the brother or sister. Yet this is not the same thing that many moral thinkers mean when they speak of the primacy of "inner intention." In their thought, the idea is that if one's desire is that good may come of one's acts, if one wishes to honor God, or if one is unselfish, then any action, including killing, can be right. But here the key "intention" is measured by the *other person*. One cannot even worship God, the text goes on to say, without being reconciled to the brother or sister. Jesus does not contrast the prohibition of killing on one hand and the love of neighbor on the other, so that for the sake of the principle of neighbor love one could kill. Jesus rather fulfills the intent of the prohibition of killing by centering it — not, as in Genesis 9, in the ritual sanctity of blood, nor, as in humanist philosophy, in the absolute value of the person — but in the fellowship between human and human, as a mirror and as means of fellowship with God....

Nonresistance is right, in the deepest sense, not because it works, but because it anticipates the triumph of the Lamb that was slain.

The apparent complicity with evil, which the nonresistance position involves, has always been a stumbling block to non-pacifists. Here we must point out that this attitude, leaving evil free to be evil, leaving the sinner free to separate himself from God and sin against humans, is part of the nature of *agape* itself, as revealed already in creation. If the cutting phrase of Péguy, *complice, c'est pire que coupable,* were true, then God himself must needs be the guilty one for making humans free and again for letting his innocent Son be killed. The modern tendency to equate involvement with guilt should have to apply *par excellence,* if it were valid at all, to the implication of the all-powerful God in the sin of his creatures. God's love for men begins right at the point where he permits sin against himself and against humans, without crushing the rebel under his own rebellion. The word for this is divine *patience,* not complicity.

But this gracious divine patience is not the complete answer to evil. We have seen that evil is already brought into check by the reign of Christ; the consummation of this reign is the defeat of every enemy by the exclusion of evil. Just as the doctrine of creation affirms that God made humans free and the doctrine of redemption says this freedom of sin was what led *agape* to the cross, so also the doctrine of hell lets sin free, finally and irrevocably, to choose separation from God. Only by respecting this freedom to the bitter end can love give meaning to history; any universalism that would seek, in the intention of magnifying redemption, to deny to the unrepentant sinner the liberty to refuse God's grace would in reality deny that human choice has any real meaning at all. With judgment and hell the old aeon comes to its end (by being left to itself) and the fate of the disobedient is exclusion from the new heaven and new earth, the consummation of the new society which began in Christ.

— *The Original Revolution*, 38–39, 41–42, 45–51, 61–62

THE FREEDOM OF THE HUMAN

The Bible sees humans as always in a context of choice. Even though many aspects of a person's situation are causally determined without his or her consent, a person is nevertheless always faced by God's "Thou shalt" and "Thou shalt not." Unless these commands of God are nonsense (which existentialism winds up affirming), they mean that humans are really placed before a decision, that they are free to choose to obey or disobey. That they will afterwards be able to analyze their decisions as having been caused makes no difference; at the time of choice, when humans face God's command and can obey or disobey, they know themselves free.

The use of the term "freedom" is a philosophical one. When the Bible says freedom it means something different, namely, redemption, freedom from sin (and *not*, as Luther, Barth, and the Neo-orthodox claim, freedom from ethical norms). The term is nonetheless clear, and the only one available, and we shall continue to use it, conscious of its shortcomings. Human freedom, as here spoken of, means that, in the context of choice before God, which is the condition of humanity, both obedience and disobedience are real possibilities.

This real freedom is at the root of all the world's troubles, and of most of theology's troubles as well. So it is that most theologies try to deny it, as do most social strategies. Only God himself, in fact, really respects this freedom.

The clearest example of theology's denial of freedom is universalism, which amounts to saying that when we think we are in a context of choice, we are not. We think ourselves free to turn away from God, but if we try it, we find ourselves roped in after all. The appearance of freedom is thus but a farce, and both human history and God's command a mockery. This is not God's way; it is a human attempt to solve a problem by defining it out of the way.

The problem of evil can be traced no further back than this; the possibility of disobedience is the sole condition for the reality of human freedom and personality. Why then did God take the risk when it would have been so easy, so much simpler, not to have created the problem? He could have run humans through their paces and never needed to atone for them. Stated this way, the question is clearly out of order, if not sacrilegious. The only answer is that God is *agape* and *agape respects the freedom of the beloved.*

This last statement is the one solid point where no exceptions may be made; it is the starting point of theology, of history, of ethics, of church order, of every realm where *agape* matters. *Agape* respects the freedom of the beloved even to lose himself. The first revelation of *agape* was thus the creation of human freedom; and no theology or ethics that denies this freedom can be true — universalism denying a human's freedom to turn away from God, Constantinianism denying the freedom not to be a Christian, monism denying humanity's real existence, totalitarianism and utopianism denying the freedom of choice (and sin) in society — for each such system denies the problem it set out to solve.

God takes the risk of leaving humans free; this is the definition of *agape* that lies at the bottom of all meaningful thought. That this lets the problem of evil in by the back door is too bad, but there was no other way, and God took that risk, precisely because of his *agape*.

— "A Study in the Doctrine of the Work of Christ," 6–7

THE DIFFERENCE
BETWEEN CHRISTIAN ETHICS
AND THE ETHICS OF THE STATE

The difference between Christian ethics for Christians and a Christian ethic for the state is therefore due to duality, not of realms or levels, but of responses. Where God speaks to the reconciled and committed believer, the command to "be minded as it befits someone who is in Christ" (Phil. 2:5) takes into consideration all the possibilities of the Holy Spirit and the church. When God's will is communicated to humans in their rebellion, neither God nor his ultimate will changes, but his current demands take into account the nonbelief of the addressee (just as any truly personal communication encounters the addressee where he or she is) and therefore stay within other limits of possibility....

Since we cannot say that God has any "proper" pattern in mind to which unbelief should conform, the Christian witness to the state will not be guided by an imagined pattern of ideal society such as is involved in traditional conceptions of the "just state," the "just war," or "the due process of law." An ideal or even a "proper" society in a fallen world is by definition impossible. The Christian speaks not of how to describe and then to seek to create the ideal society, but of how the state can best fulfill its responsibilities in a fallen society.

The Christian witness will therefore always express itself in terms of specific criticisms, addressed to given injustices in a particular time and place, and specific suggestions for improvements to remedy the identified abuse. This does not mean that

if the criticisms were heard and the suggestions put into practice, the Christian would be satisfied; rather, a new and more
demanding set of criticisms and suggestions would then follow. There is no level of attainment to which a state could
rise, beyond which the Christian critique would have nothing
more to ask; such an ideal level would be none other than the
kingdom of God.

Traditional social ethics attempted to apply principles that it
was held were somehow built into the nature of humanity or
of the social order. The approach sketched above will need to
operate without such principles, not because definite and know-
able understandings of God's will do not exist, but because such
insights are known only in Christ and their application is therefore possible only mediately. Consequently, our speaking to the
state will call for the use of middle axioms. These concepts will
translate into meaningful and concrete terms the general relevance of the lordship of Christ for a given social ethical issue.
They mediate between the general principles of Christological
ethics and the concreteness of political application. They claim
no metaphysical status, but serve usefully as rules of thumb to
make meaningful the impact of Christian social thought.

Social-ethical thought has in the past tended to sway between
a relativism that challenges the existence of any standards beyond the good intention of the person making a decision and a
natural law concept that supposes we can know clearly a pattern of ideal order that it is our assignment to impose on our
society. The conception of middle axioms avoids these alternatives. It permits meaningful communication of a significant
Christian social critique without involving extended speculation
about the metaphysical value of the principles appealed to....

The fact that the Christian social critique is therefore always
relative means that it is always misunderstood when either its
friends or its adversaries attempt to carry it to its logical conclusion. Since the Christian social critique finds its standards
in the kingdom of God — for there are no other standards —
the logical conclusion of their consistent application would be

the kingdom; but the whole reason for our present discussion is the fact that the kingdom is not an available possibility, lying beyond both the capacities and intentions of fallen society. To ask, therefore, "Where could this lead?" is to distort the nature of the problem. The fact that the world to which we speak is in rebellion guarantees that the Christian social critique can never lead too far. The world can be challenged, at the most, on one point at a time, to take one step in the right direction, to approximate in a slightly greater degree the righteousness of love.   — *The Christian Witness to the State*, 32–33, 39

THE NATIONALIST TEMPTATION

Professor James Smiley in his *Christian Church and National Ethos* details embarrassingly the extent to which America has become for its citizens a substitute church. It is from the nation and not the church that humans expect salvation in history. It is not the church but the Federal Bureau of Investigation that people are willing to trust to investigate one another's moral character and to decide who is and is not in the community. Now, if our hope is that of the American religion, it will be appropriate for our churches to strengthen the moral conviction of our civilization by having nothing to say but "God Bless America." Similarly, if our hope were that of Marxism, then we would believe that it is through our party's taking over the reins of society that the meaning of history will find its fulfillment. Then our hope for the world would appropriately include the need to rule the world and make every kind of compromise, concession, and strategic zigzag that is needed for the party to achieve this end.

The Christian community is the only community whose social hope is that we need not rule because Christ is Lord. Such hope then goes into the substance of social ethics to affirm that because it is from the cross that he reigned, because it is "the Lamb what was slain that is worthy to receive power," therefore our faithfulness and the triumph of God in human history are not linked by the mode of direct cause and effect. We do not sight down the line of our faithfulness to his triumph. We do not say that if we behave thus and so the mechanism of society will bring about this and that effect, and the result will be this desirable development or the containing of that particular evil. There is not that kind of mechanically imaged relationship between our obedience and God's fulfillment. Because therefore our hope is in Christ, the prophetic originality that the church must represent in the world is not simply that she has a more sacred cause for the sake of which she can worthily push people around. It is rather that she has a cause that dispenses her — enjoins her — from pushing people around in unworthy ways. The "otherness of the church," toward the discovery of which Christians in our age are moving on several paths, is therefore the test of the clarity of her commitment to a servant Lord.

— The Original Revolution, 118–20

BEING HONEST ABOUT JUST WAR

Counter to the standard history, the just-war position is not the one that has been taken practically by most Christians since Constantine. Most Christians (baptized people) in most wars since pacifism was forsaken have died and killed in the light of thought patterns derived from the crusade or the national-interest pattern. Some have sought to cover and interpret this activity with the rhetoric of the just-war heritage; others have not bothered. The just-war tradition remains prominent as a consensus of the stated best insights of a spiritual and intellectual elite, who used that language as a tool for moral leverage on sovereigns for whom the language of the gospel carried no conviction. Thus just-war rhetoric and consistent pacifism are on the same side of most debates. When honest, both will reject most wars, most causes, and most strategies being prepared and implemented. . . .

Not only was the just-war tradition not really in charge in history, but it was not dominant in spirituality. When a history of thought is based on the writings of a magisterial elite, then it is the just-war tradition that we must report. But how many people like that were there, and how many more drew spiritual sustenance from them?

If, on the other hand, we were to ask how through the centuries most people — who were at the same time somehow authentic Christian believers and lived their lives of faith with some explicit sincerity — thought about war, then we should have to report that their lives were sincerely burdened, not nourished, by the just-war grid. Their lives were nourished, not by the summas of the academicians, but by the lives of the saints. Most of the martyr-saints were expressly nonviolent. The rejection of violent self-defense or of service in the armies of Caesar was sometimes the reason for which the saint was martyred. The lives of the saints are told to incite the hearer to trust God for his or her surviving and prospering. Even those saints (like Francis) who lived in the midst of war and the few who were soldiers were not Machiavellian. They cultivated a worldview marked by trusting God for survival, a willingness to suffer rather than to sin, and an absence of any cynical utilitarianism in their definition of the path of obedience. The penitent and the pilgrim were normally naturally defenseless. The stories of the saints abound in tales of miraculous deliverance from the threats of bandits and brigands.

It is a source of deep historical confusion to identify the history of Christian morality as a whole with the record of the thought of academic moralists, where just-war thought in Christendom has been located. Such academic formulations may, in some cultures, make a major contribution to how people will actually make decisions in the future, *if* local preachers or confessors take their cues from the professor. But in other traditions, where the instrument of enforcement that the confessional provides is not used, the relations between the academic articulation and the real life of the community is more like that of the froth to the beer.

— *When War Is Unjust*, 68–70

THE IMPORTANCE
OF MEDIEVAL PACIFISM

There are two focal ideas in late medieval pacifism: imitation of
Jesus and law.

Imitation of Jesus

One medieval form of imitation of Jesus was the discipline of
renouncing property. The monk was a mendicant, living from
gifts rather than by working. Asceticism was the renunciation
of comfort, pride, and power. The renunciation of violence was
part of this larger withdrawal from the cares and bondages of
the world. This position, by definition, cannot be taken by all
Christians, because mendicants live in symbiotic dependency on
wider society, on the economy and generosity of others. This
kind of imitation was naïve and symbolic, though not in a
pejorative sense. It was not derived from a systematic intellectual analysis. It unfolded not from a clearly programmed vision
for how to have a different world but from prior dispositions
to challenge and undo what had cheapened Christianity since
Constantine, and from a desire to restore the normativeness
of Jesus.

When I say this rejection is symbolic, I mean that it was not
thought through in terms of social science or institutional theory. It fixed on outward expressions that represent the heart
of what had happened. The Franciscan radical went barefoot
because Jesus did not wear boots. He celebrated creation (and
criticized urbanization) by singing to the sun and talking to the
birds. He dramatized the meaning of the incarnation by con-
structing a manger scene. Poor people in the twelfth century
understood more of that symbol than we do; for us the manger
scene is romantic and cute, but they knew that to be born in
a barn is no dignity or comfort. These elements of Franciscan
asceticism and imitation led to the rejection of violence. Francis-
cans rejected violence in a way that does not convince modern
moralists, but it was convincing in the twelfth and thirteenth

centuries. Jesus was the model in his renunciation of power, pride, stability, popularity, comfort, adequate food, rest, and also violence.

Law

A second emphasis of medieval pacifism was law. Law now has a bad reputation in Protestantism, and even within Catholicism, as Catholics catch up with Protestant hangups. In order to understand what the Waldenses, or Czech Brethren, meant when they claimed to root their lives in the law of Christ or in the "minor precepts," we must make an effort at cultural reconstruction. In addition to what they called the major precepts — the Ten Commandments and the two great commandments, loving God and neighbor — these believers found six additional instructions in Matthew 5. In the late Middle Ages, these were called the minor precepts. People debated about whether they were binding. Many said that the minor precepts are merely parables or pastoral applications, illustrations, or "counsel," but unlike the major precepts, they are not simply rules to be obeyed. Medieval pacifists, however, argued that the minor precepts offer guidance that Jesus gave for us to follow. Jesus taught these things. They have the form of precepts. If Jesus is truly the Son of God, then the precepts he gave must be valid precepts. These laws are to be kept. Therefore these instructions on loving the enemy, renouncing the oath, turning the other cheek, and renouncing divorce and remarriage are binding for Christians.

The argument that law is an inadequate basis for Christian morality has been stated in various ways. Lutheranism has made one understanding clear and present in our minds. Contemporary cultural developments have raised more objections from the perspectives of psychology, pedagogy, cultural relativism, and our endemic anti-Semitism. We must not permit our embarrassment over moral rules to stand in the way of understanding the Middle Ages. Law was the way people then talked about morality. If we want to understand how the

medieval church could remain largely pacifist, despite exceptions for princes and soldiers, we must rehabilitate the notion
of law. A partial answer is that the moral reasoning of ordinary
people and priests was still on the level of legal application of
the New Testament's moral guidance.

The social critique described here became more visible in the
second millennium, and it did not begin at the point of war. It
rather began at the point of wealth, pomp, power, pride, and
simony. Simony is the sin of paying for ecclesiastical office for
economic gain. Simony was criticized with more clarity, because
the phenomenon became widespread. People acquired significant financial gain by holding church offices, especially the
office of bishop. It made sense in financial terms to bribe the
people who would elect the next bishop. Beginning in the tenth
century, a movement called Christ's Poor arose and criticized
the clergy's wealth. Christ's Poor is the historian's designation
for a host of phenomena that popped up in various places in
northern Italy and southern France which gradually led, at the
end of the twelfth century, to the movements of Peter Waldo
and Francis of Assisi.

The critique of violence was present by implication, but only
by implication. It was not spelled out or stated in theory and
was not necessarily decided on in practice. In these relatively
primitive times, the notion of religious establishment underlined
the problem, and underlay it. The question whether the Christian could be a ruler if he took Jesus seriously was present, but
only under the surface. Questions about baptizing infants or
about who is a Christian were intrinsically present, but they
were not spelled out consciously. No free church alternative
was developed in this period, although the critique that eventually led in the direction of the free churches was beginning to
percolate.

We have said what we can say to locate the pacifism of
the main stream of the medieval church. It persisted despite
Constantine and despite concessions to accommodate soldiers.
Soldiers were a small minority, and the concessions made to
accommodate them did not apply to most of the time to

most people and therefore did not immediately change the popular ethos.

— *Christian Attitudes to War, Peace, and Revolution,* 134–36

WAR AS A QUESTION
OF SPIRITUALITY

Spirituality labels for some the weight of the more-than-rational dimensions of personal experience. For others it points toward more-than-human dimensions of personal experience. For still others it pushes us to ask about the moral import of things believers do, such as praying, or breaking bread together, or forgiving. These matters do not correlate in a one-to-one way with the sides of the debate between peace churches and mainstream churches, but they tend to be weightier on the antiwar side. I shall not pursue them further here, but they would not be ignored in an adequate review.

Hugh Barbour's exposition of the subjective religious experience of radical Puritanism in England, under the heading "The Terror and Power of the Light," interprets profoundly the rootage of the renunciation of violence in the inner experience of overpowering grace. What the Anabaptists of the sixteenth century called *Gelassenheit,* or what the early Dunkards called "perfect love," or what frontier farmer preachers of the nineteenth century called "humility," or what their Wesleyan contemporaries called "sanctification," represent closely related but distinguishable labels for the view of human dignity that frees the believer from temptations to feel called to set the world right by force. Probably this commonality is more important subjectively for the peace churches' peace witness than any of the more standard ethical issues I was reviewing before.

The changes I have noted in the conversational scene are those that first come to mind, those most closely related to the classical dialectic between the peace church stance and the mainstream. There would be others, especially as the world changes: replacing the nuclear threat of the superpowers with that of rogue nations, replacing imperial outreach with the ethnic breakup of the USSR, Yugoslavia, and of smaller multicultural nations, replacing the instantaneous destruction of cities with the gradual hunting-down of peasants one village at a time that our technicians have come to call "low-intensity warfare." Concern for ecology, for the epistemological privilege of the poor, for the retrieval of indigenous cultural legacies, and for the dismantling of patriarchal cultural patterns, all have some potential for changing the shape of the conversation. At the same time, other developments continue to drive in the other direction: most notably the renewal of hostilities derived from ethnic self-understandings and reactionary appeals to religion, but also the escalating manipulative powers of money, industry, and propaganda. As far as I can see, these great changes in the dialogical setting complicate the debate since they leave some of our traditional vocabulary behind, but they do not change the basic issues.

—*The War of the Lamb*, 106–7

IS PEACE ALL OF A PIECE?

Now pacifists do vary in their views on spanking children. But practical pacifists all agree that it is simply silly to refuse to recognize the significant qualitative differences that distinguish from one another the several kinds of power. Power, even if it be called "coercive," is of a personal, humane kind as long as the individuals toward whom it is directed are conceived of as persons and their life is protected. The pressures of education, gossip, excommunication, or ostracism are still personal and permit the one against whom they are directed to be restored to the community. The power of office in business, school, or church, or even in nonlethal state functions, can be disciplined by the objectives of those institutions.

This personal quality may perhaps be retained by some exercise of police power. However, it certainly is abandoned in some other kinds of policing and utterly forsaken in war. To argue that "the problem of power is all of one piece" is possible logically, but it gives the common abstraction "power" priority over more significant variables. It is something like saying it is inconsistent for humans to practice contraception if they don't keep their dandelions from breeding, since "the problem of sexual reproduction is all of a piece."

— *Nevertheless,* 44–45

REORIENTING THE DISCUSSION ABOUT THE CHRISTIAN AND WAR

It is easy to distort the discussion about the Christian and war by transmuting it into a comparison of ethical systems. . . .

Since post-Niebuhrian nonpacifists reject pacifism, they see all pacifism as utopian purism or as withdrawal, rather than recognizing a respectable pacifist argument when presented in their own terms. The advocates of situation ethics reject pacifism for its inflexible principles. They do not bother to take seriously those pacifisms that calculate carefully in the situation, or that preserve the integrity of the loving disposition of free decision in every context.

In such cases, in other words, people are not really discussing war; they are talking past each other out of logically incompatible prior assumptions about whether and how one can think morally at all. Each kind of pacifist position has its rootage in a wider context and should be fairly evaluated in that frame of reference. . . .

The argument around pacifism is only one of the points where the multiplicity of our models of ethical thought become manifest. Academic Protestant ethical thought in mid-century was largely dominated by the social-responsibility models of the brothers H. Richard and Reinhold Niebuhr. Academic Catholic thought was comparably dominated by older principle-application models and by the changes in those patterns arising out of internal self-criticism.

New approaches to the problem of war played only a small role in those developments. That has begun to change in both families, and there have been rapprochements and overlappings among the denominational worlds (including the evangelicals and the philosophers, not mentioned above) which cannot be reviewed here. Only for a few of these developments has the issue of war been part of the picture.

Does not the manifold diversity of the approaches call us to a less monochromatic practice of ethical theologizing? Each of these logics has its own integrity. Must we seek to boil each type of pacifism down to where we can call it an inferior version of some other approach? . . .

My first plea is thus that each type of pacifist reasoning be respected in its own right. From that, it should not be inferred that a position that holds purely to one of these "types" will be more worthy of respect, or more effective, than one that blends them. I admit that in some cases mixing the modes may make for serious moral or practical confusion, especially when pragmatic arguments or just-war reasoning are interlocked with some of the others.

Nevertheless, it may well be the case that a position that weaves together more than one compatible strand will be more convincing, more effective, and more viable. Examples might be the positions of Martin Luther King Jr., of the Catholic Worker, and of Anabaptism. Here are fabrics where the several strands reinforce one another.   —*Nevertheless*, 139–41

WHAT WOULD YOU DO?

Christian love of the enemy goes beyond the bounds of decent humanism.

Any respectable person will try to treat one's neighbor as one wishes to be treated oneself. This is true simply out of recipro-cal self-interest. It is also part of one's self-respect to discipline oneself by this standard and thus rise above the level of simple retaliation.

But Jesus goes well beyond this kind of moral superiority. In his own life and career and in his instructions to his disciples, the enemy becomes a privileged object of love. We confess that the God who has worked out our reconciliation in Christ is a God who loves his enemies at the cost of his own suffering. Hence, we are to love our enemies beyond the extent of our capacity to be a good influence on them or to call forth a reciprocal love from them. In other ethical systems, the "neighbor" may well be dealt with as an object of our obligation to love. But Jesus goes further and makes of our relation to the adversary the special test of whether the love we have is derived from the love of God.

This is counter to the general assumption that Jesus simply restated the law's command to "love your neighbor as yourself." Instead, Jesus' "new commandment" was that his disciples should love as he loved — or as God loved them. "Love your neighbor as yourself" is the center not of Jesus' teaching but of the law which he fulfills and transcends.

So the answer for the Christian to the "what if...?" question is this: I seek to deal with the aggressor as God in Christ has dealt with me — or as I would wish to be dealt with. The capacity for this simple act is not dependent on being able to "put one's mind to it" and think through the options. In fact, thinking through the options may make obedience harder. The simple, loving Christian may never have thought through the situation but still responds out of God's love for oneself. Such a believer may well be nearer to obedience than those of us who think we must logically process the kinds of concerns about which I have just written.

The Christian's loyalty to the bonds of social unity is loosened by the decision to follow Christ.

In various statements recorded in the gospels, Jesus called his disciples to forsake not only houses and land but even father and mother, spouse and child. Any consideration of what this means must at least make us question the assumption that the first test of moral responsibility or of virility is the readiness to kill in defense of one's family.

The great Luther hymn "A Mighty Fortress" states this, in English translation: "Let goods and kindred go; this mortal life also." The German is more dramatic: "They seize wife and child; let it take its course!" This is not mere poetic exaggeration. Martin Luther taught nonresistance on the personal level. He believed that violence was permissible only at the behest of a legitimate government in a just cause.

The Christian's understanding of the resurrection of the dead, of heaven and hell, and of eternal life — all this informs the approach to the "what if...?" situation.

We've already conceded that the classic Christian understanding of Providence might not be accepted by modern debaters. The same is true of classical Christian understandings of a transcendent life. We cannot impose such conceptions upon modern challengers. Yet at least we can ask those within historic Christianity to understand that our beliefs may reinforce our readiness to accept the cost of obedience when confronted by a hostile aggressor.

Consider the belief that there is such a thing as hell, some kind of extension or reaffirmation beyond death of the meaning of life, in which one's fate or state is conditioned by the self-centered, shallow kind of life one has been leading. I can ask my challenger to acknowledge that on the basis of such a belief, it would be most likely that my killing the attacker would seal for him that negative destiny. I would take away from him any possibility of repentance and faith. I would be doing this in order to save from death someone who — pardon the piety, but it is a meaningful Christian stance — is "ready to meet her Maker." To keep out of heaven temporarily someone who wants to go there ultimately anyway, I would consign to hell immediately someone whom I am in the world to save.

Committed Christians see in their life of faith not merely an ethical stance in which they want to be consistent, nor a set of rules they want to be sure not to break, but a gracious privilege which they want to share.

They guide their lives not so much by "How can I avoid doing wrong?" or even "How can I do the right?" as by "How can I be a reconciling presence in the life of my neighbor?" From this perspective, I might justify firm nonviolent restraint, but certainly never killing. Most of the time the committed Christian testifies, at least in theory, that God intervenes in the lives of selfish creatures to change those lives, and that he does so through his children. When is that testimony tested more than when I am invited to act toward an aggressor as though there can be for him no change of heart?

For the Christian, to bear the martyr's cross is to share in God's way with his world.

The New Testament and much later Christian testimony indicate that martyrdom is in some sense a normal path that at least some Christians need to follow at least sometimes. How then could I possibly be led along the path of innocent suffering if my pragmatic managing of the "what if . . . ?" situation determines this as the one thing that I must not let happen?

Christian faith warns me that I tend to use self-centered control of my decision as a tool of rebelliousness to solidify my independence from my Maker.

We've already noted the moral limits of a self-centered decision-making process. But Christian faith goes much further. Common sense tells us that people tend to be selfish and allow their selfishness to influence their perception. Christian thought goes on to label as "pride" that rebellious autonomy on which I insist despite the fact that ultimately, if not overcome by God's grace, it means my own destruction.

Common sense says that any person is limited in the capacity to observe and evaluate the facts by a particular point of view and the limits of vision. But Christian faith tells me, in addition, that my selfish mind, my impatient and retaliating spirit, and my adrenalin — these all negatively warp the way I perceive the facts to make them reflect my self-esteem and my desire to be independent of my Creator at the cost of my neighbor. Thus common sense argues for modesty about my capacity to make valid decisions by myself. However, the Christian understanding of sin goes well beyond that to call me to repent of the very idea that I might make a decision completely on my own.

The real temptation of "good" people like us is not the crude, the crass, and the carnal. The really refined temptation, with which Jesus himself was tried, is that of egocentric altruism. It is to claim oneself to be the incarnation of a good and righteous cause for which others may rightly be made to suffer. It is stating one's self-justification in the form of a duty to others.

— *What Would You Do?* 38–42

WHAT SEEMS GOOD
TO THE HOLY SPIRIT

One early summary statement of this empowerment is the word of Jesus in the gospel of John: "...it is to your advantage that I go away, for if I do not go away, the Advocate will not come to you; but if I go, I will send him to you.... When the Spirit of truth comes, he will guide you into all the truth" (16:7, 12).

That promised guide, the Holy Spirit, will operate in the community to make present, for hitherto unforeseen times and places and questions, the meaning of the call of Jesus. It uses a fully human communication process, called by the rabbis "binding and loosing." It has about it elements of what today would be called conflict resolution. It gathers up the resources of human wisdom, the perspectives of several kinds of involvement in different ways of perceiving a question, and loving processes of negotiation, all of this guided and enabled by God's own presence.

Any "social ethic" in the ordinary sense of the term, any *full* system of goals and procedures, that could be adequate to guide the obedience of Christians in one specific situation, would by that very fact have to be out of date or out of place in other situations. When, on the other hand, the guidance we have is constitutional or procedural, any new situation can be met with the resources of valid community process.

The guidance is not only procedural; there are substantial prescriptions as well. We are told to tell the truth, to keep promises, and to care for the needy. Yet the point at which the divine empowerment is crucial has to do not so much with identifying the initial sources of the substantial guidance — the rules to apply — in this or that set of revelatory propositions, as with trusting the Spirit's leading in contextual application.

The conclusion of the Jerusalem conferences of Acts 15:28, "It has seemed good to the Holy Spirit and to us," is presented by the author of Acts as a model for valid process.

— Body Politics, 8–9

In the New Testament, teaching and testing were defined functions necessary in the church. The New Testament church did not assume that the truth was all in the teachings of Jesus or in the teachings about Jesus. It is assumed that truth will continue to come and that new revelations, new workings of the Spirit, will continue. They are expected of the prophets in Acts. They are still expected in the prophets of the post-canonical *Didache.* They are expected in 1 Corinthians 14 as a normal function of the church's life, but they must be tested. No one thought the truth was all settled.

As the church continues to meet new challenges, speak new languages, and enter new cultures in the leading of the Holy Spirit, she always makes new statements she claims are true, but then they have to be tested. They are tested by their link to the core message, the Jesus story. Then they are tested by their relationship to the wider body of primitive traditions, like the gospels. Then they can begin to be tested by the way the New Testament church read the Old Testament, looking behind itself to find its face there. Then we begin to be able to test them by the coherent systematic thought of three great theologians of the New Testament. The church moved on from there, but this process of testing established the canonical body of statements to which we can go back as a point of reference.

— Preface to Theology, 379–80

Throughout the Israelite story, the activities of prophets, judges, and "the elders in the gate" relativized the centrality of the

ritual life although they still honored it. After the end of kingship and the loss of the Jerusalem temple, Jewry survived not
by creating a surrogate for the Temple so as to keep using the
priesthood, but by inventing a new role, that of the rabbi, stew-
ard of the Torah, and a new social instrument, the synagogue,
formed of any ten households, with no religious specialist
needed in their midst at all.

By the time of Jesus, the Temple with its priesthood had been
restored, but he relativized it again. He formed a movement out
of fishermen, zealots, and publicans — and women — sending
seventy of them (the same number as Moses) out across the
countryside. That set the stage for the qualitatively new impact
of the Christian movement, as interpreted in the Pauline texts
we have been reading. Among the first Christians at Jerusalem
were some priests who continue to take their turns at officiat-
ing in the Temple, but they had no priestly role in the messianic
synagogues because there was no sacrificial worship there. The
specialized purveyor of access to the divine is out of work since
Pentecost.

Sometimes the early Christians said they were all priests;
sometimes they said that the priesthood was done away with.
The concrete social meanings of the two statements, though verbally opposite, were the same. All members of the body alike
are Spirit-empowered. The monopoly of the sacrificial celebration that enables and delimits human access to the divine is
swept away. The priestly person as the primary agent of access
to the divine is swept away with the special ceremonies. Jesus
was the last sacrifice and thus he was also the last priest. The
antipriestly impact of this change, although expressed emphat-
ically in the Pauline writings and in Hebrews, is one of the
dimensions of redemption least noted and least honored in
Christian history since then.

Soon, as we have already seen, the sweeping Pauline vision
was lost. Because no central authority existed in the early
churches, it probably never generally won out in the first
place. The notion that there are several ministries remained
for a while — deacon and deaconess, lector, exorcist — but the

conviction that *every* member of the body is charismatically empowered for a nameable role was soon lost. We need not ask whether the "blame" for this loss should be assigned to a resurgence of patriarchal social habits or to the assimilation of pagan notions of sacrificial cult or to certain threats of disorder that someone felt a need to ward off or to the domination of later generations by the habits of churches that had never heard or accepted the Pauline message in the first place. We often forget that what we call the New Testament canon was not that for two centuries.

Still later, the restored monopoly of the priestly role was reinforced by its alliance with the sacral notion of kingship, renewed in the fourth century by Constantine.

In any case, Paul's vision has yet to be consciously and consistently lived out. In various renewal movements over the centuries there has been *some* sense of lay empowerment and decentralized accountable leadership, but it seldom lasts long. It is seldom thought through as an intentional part of the reformation project. Although the Friends, the Plymouth Brethren, and the Salvation Army have come closer than most Protestants to relativizing the priestly monopoly and validating varied ministries, even they did not set out to realize what Paul had written about. It happened to them, as they were being led by the Spirit on other fronts, that they found God empowering nonclergy, including women, and they honored these gifts, but they did not generalize. Something of this is happening again today in the "base communities" of Latin America, but again without being programmatically intended.

Although Paul's warrant for his exhortation is derived from the order of redemption, his vision of complementary functions, working together after the model of the several members of the human organism, is applicable to any organization with complex tasks. The modern notions of teamwork, which I argued above are not the source of Paul's vision, are in fact reflections or spin-offs from it. It enables the detailed analysis of the several functional components of any task so that each can be most appropriately discharged. It enables the factory system, the research team, the university, and the city. It explains why factories and businesses where every worker participates in policy making and quality control can make better automobiles or sell more software than those whose organization is vertical.

— *Body Politics*, 56–58

THE POWER OF TRUTH
AS FORCE

One component of Gandhi's vision that moves with Tolstoy, but beyond him, is that he understands more realistically the power of truth as force. Tolstoy affirmed that the course of human history was carried by suffering but could not explain how. Gandhi's vision of the cosmos as a unity of spiritual powers, interwoven in an unbroken net of causation, made sense out of the notion that fasting or praying or sexual continence, and above all the active renunciation of violence, could exert spiritual power — "soul force" — upon the adversary one desires not to destroy but to restore to a fuller human community. Had Gandhi been more versed in New Testament theology, he might have spoken of such a power in terms of the *logos* sustaining all of creation or of the risen Lord subjecting to his sovereignty the powers of a rebellious creation. It was simpler for him to understand the efficacy of renunciation in more Indian terms. Thus the first stage of deepening in the transition from Tolstoy to Gandhi is a more transparent cosmological account of how suffering "works."

The other side of that same progress is the development of social strategies that fit the cosmology. Out of the religious holiday of *hartal* develops the work stoppage; out of purity rituals, the boycott. Going to jail for refusal to obey an unjust law places moral pressure upon the judge and thereby upon the legislator (especially in a democratic society). The illegitimate assembly, the procession or march provokes the oppressor to unveil his illegitimacy by lashing out and seizes the attention of the public, including the newspaper readers of London.

Gandhi has added to Tolstoy's spiritual diagnosis both philosophical clarity and organizational genius. The organizational insights arose slowly and were practiced before they were understood. They were:

(a) The social basis in a communal farm/school/retreat center (the *Ashram*)

(b) The appropriation of traditional religious forms (the fast, the procession, regular daily prayers)

(c) A thoroughly popular form of journalism, eschewing any complex theory (Gandhi's writing is brief, epigrammatic, repetitive)

(d) The appeal to the positive values of Anglo-Saxon law, both to the citizen's rights and the independence of the courts

(e) The commitment that the adversary is to be won over, yet not defeated

(f) The interpretation of civil disobedience not as obstruction or coercion but as obedience to a higher power and as refusal to cooperate in one's own oppression

(g) A strong sense of fair play (Gandhi refused to press his advantage to demand more than the original goals of an action, and he would not undertake an action when the authorities were under attack from another quarter)

(h) Rigorous self-discipline (Gandhi would terminate a popular action if its nonviolent discipline broke down)

(i) An alternative social vision (Gandhi called it the "constructive program," and he had no interest in simply replacing English oppression, capitalism, and urbanization with Indian oppression)

(j) A readiness to take positions unpopular with his own people (Gandhi criticized untouchability and Hindu-Muslim enmity).

— *Nonviolence*, 24–26

THE IMPORTANCE OF
THE CULTIVATION OF VIRTUE

Another classical pattern of moral reasoning in Roman Catholicism has always been *the cultivation of virtue.* This is a very different focus of attention from the absolute law of God, yet it has in common with that approach a relative unconcern for pragmatic measurement of the situation. A Christian, by nature, is meek, or is ready to suffer, or is a servant, or is nonviolent. The true Christian is one for whom the cultivation of that character is a dominant commitment that effectively determines her or his way of living and being.

It is obvious that this concentration upon the Christian life as a matter of quality rather than impact is most at home within the disciplined religious life. That makes it easy for Protestants to disqualify it as not involved with the real world, or as self-righteous. Nonetheless, this heritage of religious discipline has made it possible, through the centuries, for some Catholics — despite the dominance of the just-war tradition — to have kept their minds and their elbows free to have room for the continued confession of the contemplation of the full meaning of Jesus as not only savior figure, but model.

It is by no means the case that this priority commitment to the nature of virtue must lead to social inefficacy. It involves its own style of historical impact. No one can say that St. Francis, or Dorothy Day, or Mother Teresa of Calcutta have been without social impact. Their pattern for decision making and goal setting is one that bypasses the social-mechanism models of cultural process that Western intellectuals have come to trust. In the religious community where ritual and spirituality are assumed to be as real as mechanism, this should not at all be considered a disadvantage. Thus it has been natural, and should have been no surprise, that one of the foundational components of Catholic pacifism in our time has been represented — as we shall soon see — by the proponents (or shall we say the bearers) of that redemptive qualitative understanding of nonviolence as a spiritual discipline. Nonviolence is not a negation or an absence, but an affirmation. To reject violence is to affirm or (even more actively) to defend the integrity of that which one refuses to violate even in the name of some good cause. That active renunciation of violation and defense of the potentially violated is the active translation of the ancient virtue of "meekness," that quality of self-emptying that makes one an apt subject for inheriting the earth. —*Nonviolence,* 111–12

CULTIVATING NEW SKILLS

It was the earth that received the blood of Abel, and it was the earth that was cursed for Cain. Our violence toward one another also breaks our unity with nature. Just as in Genesis the sin against God, the abuse of the tree of life, resulted in expulsion from the garden, so today the fruitfulness of the land is jeopardized by hostility between us. We notice occasionally how our society is dependent on nature, and how the shape of the soils or the snows or the floods influences our well-being, but we seldom analyze deeply enough to know how much our land is being abused in the name of our civilization. As the word indicates, *cult*ivation, what Cain was the first to do, is the first form of *cult*ure. To develop a fruitful field demands years of cooperation between the farmer and his land, his learning how to nurture it, how to adjust the crops to the soils and the calendar. Cain cannot be a farmer if he cannot be trusted with his brother's life. If we must constantly be taking refuge in the walls of cities, we cannot be out working the fields.

This offense escalates, just as we saw the offense of vengeance escalating. What the United States did to nature in Southeast Asia with defoliants and herbicides, bombs and bulldozers, was unprecedented in degree. Yet the fact that nature was the victim was not a new thing. The Thirty Years' War made some of western Europe desert for generations. The Crusades did the same thing in the Middle East. Our battleship artillery again did it to the hills behind Beirut. War always means pillage and scorched earth. The effects of a massive nuclear exchange upon our ecology will be new in degree, but we have always drawn our patient vulnerable mother earth into the suffering we inflict on our neighbors.

This is the normal extension of the curse of Cain, and specifically of the mark of Cain (the fact that he is protected by a circle of vengeance). What is destroying nature and destroying the possibility of social peace is not anarchy, but government gone beyond bounds. What is killing us is not savagery, but civilization. The saga of Genesis simply describes that fact. That is the way it is: the reciprocal interlocking of genocide and ecocide. The voice of our brothers' blood cries out to God, and we cannot live with our brother on the land. What can we do with a lost creation? What would you do? What would you try to do if you were God? . . .

Peace is something to be waged

    . . . to plan for
    . . . to train for
    . . . to sacrifice for
    . . . to die for

Peace has institutional prerequisites that don't just happen; they need to be built.

Peace has attitudinal prerequisites that run against the grain of our nationalistic and racist cultures. They can be brought about only by experiences of unlearning, relearning.

We are given glimpses of the alternative culture that the nations will create when they have come to Jerusalem.

The *first* is what we today call economic conversion. It is expressed in the phrase we know best from the prophecy: swords shall be transformed into plowshares.

The skills of smelting and smithing will be devoted no more to arming but to farming. The sharp edges will still be needed. In fact the edge of an agricultural implement needs to last longer and to cut more often than a weapon. So to make coulters instead of swords, and pruning knives instead of spears, will mean a technological advance, not a slowing down (just as today the armament industry is the least efficient and least competitive segment of the industrial economy). Thus the prophets' vision is not primitivism or "back to nature." It calls for the more expert and more productive use of the skills of smelter and smith.

The *second* change to be described is the renunciation of war as the institutional means of conflict resolution. It is not said that there will be no more nations — on the contrary. It is not said that they will have no differences, or no selfish interests. But because the Lord is their arbiter, they will make no plans for war.

Now we need to remember that war is an institution. It is not something that can happen without planning. A deed of violent *personal* self-defense may be spontaneous. A nonviolent action may sometimes be spontaneous (although the best ones are usually planned). A deed of reconciliation may be a decision of the moment (although even when such creative gestures seem to be quite spontaneous, they are most often also the product of indirect premeditation and the expression of a gradually learned lifestyle).

But a war cannot be spontaneous. It must be studied for. It is complex and costly. It demands enormous organization to do things that are not done every day. It needs skills different from those of wholesome daily life. If you don't prepare for war, you won't have war. The prophet says that they won't prepare, thereby aligning himself with the many other places in the psalms and the prophets where the end of war is announced as part of the prophets' hope.

— He Came Preaching Peace, 61–62, 99–100

THE NEW HUMANITY
AS PULPIT AND PARADIGM

Ethics is more than ethics. Actions proclaim. The new peoplehood constituted by the grace to which the readers of these texts had responded is *by its very existence* a message to the surrounding world. The medium and the message are inseparable. *What* God is doing is bringing into existence a new historic reality, a community constituted by the flowing together of two histories, one with the law and one without. *How* God is doing it is not distinguishable from *what* God is doing, and *how the world can know* about it is again the same thing....

Most of our contemporary epistemologically preoccupied thinkers, who worry about making reasonable sense to their unbelieving or otherwise-believing neighbors, would certainly deny that they hold any anti-Judaic bias. Yet it is clear that in setting up their sense of what would count as cross-cultural sense making, they are quite un-Jewish. Their grid cannot do justice to the way in which a particular faith-defined community (or, if you wish, a particular community-defined faith) has across the centuries been demonstrably larger and not smaller than the local "publics" among which it was dispersed, whether that be the Jews in Babylon in the age of Jeremiah and Ezekiel, or in Rome or Spain or Asia Minor in the age of Paul, or in Alexandria or Marseilles in the age of Constantine, or in Moscow in the age of Lenin, or in New York or Los Angeles today.

What two and a half millennia of Jewish history have demonstrated prototypically, shorter stretches of experience have exemplified again in the history of the several particular faith communities in America, be they Roman Catholic or Quaker or secularist. Only a believing community with a "thick" particular identity has something to say to whatever "public" is "out there" to address. And to repeat the vice versa from before, only the community that welcomes the challenge of public witness can justify (not merely to outsiders but also to its own children) its distinctive existence....

My metaphor of "pulpit" or "pedestal" expresses the functional necessity of just being there with a particular identity. If there had not been a critical mass of Quakers in early Pennsylvania, living out a nonviolent, dialogical lifestyle, the uniqueness of that colony in contrast to the others, with regard to religious liberty, democracy, respect for the Indians, and early challenging of slavery could not have happened. Something similar would be true of the place of Roman Catholics in early Maryland. Had there not been Catholic Worker houses since the 1930s, there could not have been a Catholic peace witness in the 1970s. Had there not been solid black Baptist and Methodist churches and colleges in the South for generations, there would not have been an effective civil rights movement beginning in the 1950s. The faith community whose vision of what they stand for is strong enough that whether they stand by it does not depend on short-range applause or success is the necessary condition for the wider witness. A moral insight that cannot survive when held to *against the stream* by tolerated but disadvantaged aliens is not worthy to be proclaimed to the public.

The second metaphor in my title is "paradigm." This points to the awareness that the way most communication works is not by projecting and then reassembling a maximum number of atoms of information, nor of axioms and maxims, but by pattern recognition. This is prototypically illustrated by five parallel phenomena that are all part of our common apostolic heritage. I last gathered them in my pamphlet *Body Politics,* but none of them is my discovery. I begin by itemizing all five without much detail. They could be listed in any order, and there could very well be a sixth or seventh.

1. The Jesus of Matthew's account twice uses the verbs "to bind" and "to loose" to denote a function that he wanted his followers to discharge in his name. It means both to forgive (or to withhold forgiveness) and to make moral decisions. It is to be done by means of person-to-person encounter, with a reconciling intention, and with Christ's own authority behind it. This model has been taken seriously in the Rule of Benedict and in the reformations called Anabaptist and Quaker and Methodist. If decision making through reconciling dialogue is the way for the people of God to define the ongoing meaning of their peoplehood, it is also the model for the ways a wider society

should make decisions and resolve conflict. In our time "conflict resolution" and "mediation" have become a part of the disciplines of sociology and psychology for interpersonal and intergroup relations; the rules are the same.

2. Jesus' disciples formed a small commune around him during his lifetime, and when after his ascension they solidified that pattern of eating together, they considered it the right way both to *remember* his death and his resurrection appearances and to *affirm their hope* of his return. Our history of centuries of speculation and controversy about what happens to bread and wine when a certain special person speaks certain special Latin words over them obscured from our memory for a long time the fact that the *primary* meaning of the eucharistic gathering in the gospels and Acts is economic. It was the fulfillment of the promise of the Magnificat that the rich would give up their advantages and the poor would be well fed. Luke's report probably is intended to signal the fulfillment of the mandate of Deuteronomy (15:4) that "there should be no poor among you." It was in order to manage this primeval socialism that the Jerusalem church first expanded its leadership to include non-Palestinian leaders, the first step (according to Acts) toward the opening to the Gentiles. In recent years various theologians have set about retrieving the paradigmatic power of the Eucharist as the grounds for the preferential option for the poor. At the Lord's Table, those who have bread bring it, and all are fed; that is the model for the Christian social vision in all times and places.

3. The term "new humanity" ... or the phrase "new creation," which has the same meaning in other epistles, means ... that Jewishness and Gentileness have flowed together in one new cultural history of salvation. But when we began I did not point out that the literary and liturgical settings in which we find these terms embedded have to do with baptism. To be "in Christ" through baptism means to have entered this new history. Interethnic reconciliation is a part of redemption. It is not a social idealism supported by an appeal to creation or reason. It is the result of the cross.

Enlightenment humanism tells a different story. According to an ancient American document, as you well know, we are supposed to hold it to be a self-evident truth that all "men" are equal by creation. We could of course dwell on more than one shortcoming of that revolutionary vision. "All men," when that declaration was trumpeted across the Atlantic in 1776, did not include women or black or red men or poor men. Nor is the *notion* of creation endowing creatures with rights self-evident. But the more fundamental error is that people are *in fact* not equal by creation. Every well-established understanding of creation in the roots of our culture has seen it as explaining not how we are the same but how we are different. Slaveholders in the antebellum South of this country, Afrikaners in the Republic of South Africa, and Ian Paisley in Belfast have all rooted their ethnic separatism in a doctrine of creation. A psychologist and social theorist have just in recent weeks sparked a new firestorm by saying it again about IQ and earning power.

According to the apostolic witness, interethnic harmony is a work not of creation but of redemption. To make anyone believe in the equal *dignity* of all humans God must intervene. It took the cross to break down the wall. In the movements of Gandhi and King it took freely chosen, innocent suffering to renew in our century the possibility of reconciliation between peoples.

4. The "Paul" of Ephesians used the term "fullness of Christ" to describe the unique social pattern that he called his readers to actualize in their common life. The earlier Paul of Romans 12 and 1 Corinthians 12 had made the same point with other language. Every person in the community has been given by the Spirit a distinctive portion of grace, which consists in a role in the community. That role can and should be named, so that the individual can be challenged to fulfill it well, and so that the community can rejoice in it and monitor its functioning. Every member of the body has a role; no role is more central than any other, and the least-honored roles should be most affirmed. The relapse of early Christianity into sacerdotal patriarchy led to the loss of this vision as a way of realistically sharing the roles

of members in community, but it has occasionally resurfaced in visions of shared ministry. Today in fact this vision is more widely operative in the rest of society than in the traditional churches, as the division of labor has enabled the culture of the university or the factory or the city.

5. The guidance Paul sent to the Corinthians about how to hold a meeting in the power of the Spirit prescribed that all present should be free to take the floor. The only authority role in the meeting would be a moderator to make sure that all get that opportunity, that they speak in turn, and that anyone speaking in another tongue be translated. In radical Protestantism, especially in Quakerism, this vision was retrieved and implemented with great creativity and thoroughness. Especially since the Puritan reformation it has reached out powerfully into the wider society in the form of town-meeting democracy and the imperative of the freedoms of assembly, speech, and the press. As I needed to say before concerning interethnic reconciliation, the basis for this freedom is not in the nature of things as they already are by nature or by creation, but in the divine intervention which we call the work of reconciliation, which ascribes status to the underdog and the outsider, loosens tongues, and opens ears. That everyone who has something to say gets a hearing is not a "given," the way things are; it is a gift which the community is enabled by the power of the Spirit to impart.

There you have before you the fivefold pattern. In each case the shape of grace is described and prescribed and practiced in the early church as a social process pattern, enabled and mandated as a part of the good news of redemption. Yet in each case that way of interacting in the faith community is so concrete, so accessible, so "lay," that it is also a model for how any society, not excluding the surrounding "public" society, can also form its common life more humanely. The church is called to live and is beginning to live (to the extent to which we get the point) in the way to which the whole world is called.

— *For the Nations,* 41–46

My earlier experience of serendipitous induction saw falling into place five distinct social practices in the early Christian church. I have exposited elsewhere the high degree of structural similarity that these practices show, even though there is nothing in the New Testament literature itself to give any indication that the writers were in touch with each other or were conscious of running through some standard outline. Again the commonality is structural, not verbal. It consists not in concepts but in practices, yet behind the practices we can discern shared understandings. That is all the more reason to take seriously the claim that the common shape has something to tell us.

It is hardly arguable in our day that a particular set of concepts that one claims to have derived from a particular text should be believed *only* because "it is in the Bible" as a special set-apart literature. That is the way the Protestant scholastic heritage is caricatured by some of its "fundamentalist" heirs, and, reacting to them, by some of its "liberal" critics. There is, however, reason to be especially attentive to messages that at first sight are counterintuitive and countercultural. Such initially unexpected testimonies merit *a priori* the benefit of the doubt. Investment in the text's own frame of reference is imperative, because only such an investment can be fair to the text's intent, especially if it is prophetic (i.e., by definition a challenge to ordinary habits of mind). This is, however, not to ask special treatment for the Bible because it is the Bible; the investment in understanding the text's intent is imperative for reading any kind of literature fairly.

Might the commonalities be the product of my biased readings, forcing the texts into my own mold? I let the reader judge. In each of the above cases I happened serendipitously upon the parallels that I observed. I was not looking for something. I am no more responsible for creating the pattern I found there than is the astronomer for creating the lines in a star's spectrum. The lines were there all the time, even though it took the telescope, the spectrometer, the photographic film, and the astronomer to "reveal" their patterns.

Might the commonalities be the banal effect of a common early Christian culture's shared assumptions? They could if their content were commonplace; yet the common testimony of the several "christological" passages was innovative and countercultural. It negated even the logic implied in the very language they borrowed. Nobody had said those things before with those words. The five "sacramental" behaviors are likewise countertraditional in the way they see human and divine action coinciding.   —To Hear the Word, 115–16

In that basic "lay" sense of a human action in which God is active, all of these five practices — fraternal admonition, the open meeting, and the diversification of gifts, no less than the other practices of baptism and Eucharist — are worship, are ministry, are doxology (praise), are celebratory, and are mandatory. They are actions of God, in and with, through and under what men and women do. Where they are happening, the people of God is real in the world.

Although atypical and nontraditional, these activities are not esoteric or difficult to understand. They are publicly accessible behaviors, which the neighbors cannot merely notice but in fact share in, understand, and imitate. Whether this means they should be called ordinances, as Baptists and Brethren prefer, or sacraments, as the "high" traditions do (but with a "low" meaning), I don't mind letting the reader decide.

There is another set of terms, of themes, to which we need also to relate our "five practices." Terms such as *spiritual discipline* have recently become familiar (or become familiar again). Modes of prayer, meditation, counseling, devotional practices, and spiritual direction, which were once automatically taken for granted in church-dominated cultures, today come to be taken up again by some as voluntary disciplines. These activities are like the ones we have been studying here, in that they make the Christian life a matter of direct attention and intention. Such disciplines certainly will support and be supported by the "five practices"; they differ in their interpersonal, even institutional concreteness.   —Body Politics, 72–73

THE EUCHARIST
AS ECONOMIC ETHICS

The Eucharist is an act of economic ethics. In the passages
to which later generations gave the technical label "words of
institution" Jesus says, "Whenever you do this, do it in my
memory." Do *what* in his memory? It cannot mean "whenever you celebrate the Mass" because there was then no such
thing as a Mass. He might mean "whenever you celebrate
the Passover," but that is not what the hearers took him to
mean. That would have called for an annual celebration. He
must have meant (and record indicates that they took him to
mean) "whenever you have your common meal." The meal he
blessed and claimed as his memorial was their ordinary partak-
ing together of food for the body. Only because it was that
communal meal of the disciples' fellowship could it provide
the occasion for their organization of the ministering structures
reported in Acts 7.

We commit the hermeneutical sin of anachronism when we
look in the New Testament for any light on the much later
eucharistic controversies. All of those later controversies were
about something of which the apostolic generation had no
notion, namely, about the detailed theoretical definition of the
meaning of specific actions and things ("sacraments") within
the special set-apart world of the "religious" in a frame of reference that the later churches took over from paganism when
the latter replaced Judaism as their cultural soil. What the
New Testament is talking about in "breaking bread" is believers actually sharing with one another their ordinary day-to-day
material substance. It is not the case, as far as understanding the New Testament accounts is concerned, that, in an
act of "institution" or symbol making, God or the church
would have said "let bread stand for daily sustenance." It is
not even merely that, in many settings, as any cultural historian would have told us, eating together already stands for
values of hospitality and community formation, these values
being distinguishable from the signs that refer to them. It is

that bread is daily sustenance. Bread eaten together *is* economic sharing. Not merely symbolically but in actual fact it extends to a wider circle the economic solidarity that normally is obtained in the family. When, in most of his post-resurrection appearances, Jesus takes the role of the family head distributing bread (and fish) around his table, he projects into the post-Passion world the common purse of the wandering disciple band whose members had left their prior economic bases to join his movement.

A rationalistic or Zwinglian understanding of symbol says that a symbolic act has a "meaning" distinguishable from the act itself and that, for certain purposes, it is in fact helpful to disentangle the "meaning" from the act. This is in order to define it, to derive from it additional derivative meanings, and perhaps to resymbolize it into other forms in other settings. In this frame of reference, one can say (although no one did for a long time) that breaking bread together *means* economic solidarity, so that forms of social life that transcend individualism and share with larger communities are preferable to those that name as agents only independent individuals. But such an action of derivation is an intellectual operation, arbitrary and unaccountable. This we might call the "Zwinglian" way of access to an economic meaning of the Eucharist.

At the other end of the scale, what we may call the "sacramentalist" view of a sign says that by a distinct divine act of definition, a specific set of practices is pulled up out of daily life and given, by gracious decree, a distinctive meaning, one best served by accentuating the distance between the special meaning and the ordinary one. A separate "theology of sacraments" then develops a corpus of dogma about that special realm. The bread no longer looks or tastes like the bread one shares with children and guests or that is owed to cousins and to the beggar. It is not broken nor (classically) even put into the mouth the same way as ordinary, real-world food. Its most important meaning is the one that forces us to debate in what sense the bread has now become the body of the Lord and in what sense our eating it mediates to us the grace of salvation. I submit that (although this is no place to spread out the argument) there is no direct path from this point to economics. The Roman Catholic authors who establish such a connection have to start over again from somewhere else.

What I propose, for present purposes, to call the sacramental (as distinct from the sacramentalistic) view spares us those abstracted definitions and articulations of how the sign signifies. When the family head feeds you at his or her table the bread for which he or she has given thanks, you are part of the family. The act does not merely *mean* that you are part of the family. To take the floor in a community dialogue does not mean that you are part of the group; it *is* operational group membership. To be immersed and to rise from the waters of the *mikvah* may be said to symbolize death and resurrection, but really it makes you a member of the historical community of the new age. This was the case, not only for Jesus, but also for John and for the other Jewish proselytizers and revivalists who used the baptism of repentance before him.   — *The Royal Priesthood,* 364–66

VOCATION

In view of the widespread impact of what is usually called the "Protestant doctrine of vocation," our review will be furthered by a detour at this point. We take note of the insufficiency of that approach in its usual form. That doctrine is a standard way in which Protestant social thought has looked at roles and institutions. It assumes that the Christian will bring to her or his "vocational" role her or his loving intention, integrity, and industriousness, and the modesty resulting from knowing he or she is a forgiven sinner, but that the *content* of one's activity in that "vocation" or "station" or "office," what the person should actually do, does not come from his or her faith in Jesus but from the "order of creation." The institutions in their present shape reveal God's will for the shape of society because

God made them that way. That is why the shape of society is called "the order of creation." Each of us is called to live up to the dictates of our "station" or role.

The service of the Christian in his or her secular role must, according to this view, be protected against any too direct carryover from the gospel. Some Lutheran theologians call this the *Eigengesetzlichkeit der Kulturgebiete* (the autonomy of each realm of culture), and some conservative Calvinists call it "sphere sovereignty." According to this "order of creation," bankers should accumulate money, not share it, as John the Baptist and Jesus told people to do; that is the meaning of banking as part of the way things just are. Lords should domineer, and soldiers and hangmen should kill, because those are their defined roles in the world. Slaves should remain slaves; women should remain subject; anyone who is under orders should respect the boss.

The natural effect of this vision of authority structures being anchored in the structures of "creation" is of course conservative and patriarchal. Its strongest voices in our time have been the Reformed rulers of South Africa and Northern Ireland. A century and a half ago in the United States, it provided the strongest argument in favor of slavery.

The gospel answer to this notion is not that there is no such thing as the Christian calling or vocation, but that it is *not* to be distinguished from or contrasted with following Jesus. The notion of an order of creation is not necessarily all wrong, but since sin came into the world we cannot discern which traits of "the way things are" are the way God wants them and which are fallen, disobedient, and oppressive.

If we are to make something of the concept of "vocation" in the light of the gospel, we must reverse those assumptions. We must undercut the individualism and the pressure to blind conformity of that view of vocation by developing strands of accountability to tie the vocational servant to various constituencies and communities, denying the sovereignty of any sphere over against the gospel.

This attention to "vocation" was something of a detour just here because it does not apply peculiarly or only to the common meal or to economic matters. It is appealed to all across the board in Christian social ethics. I have lifted it up here because the specimen of banking is an especially pertinent example. The other examples of "corrections," war, patriarchal family patterns, and (longer ago) slavery, which I have just alluded to in parallel, reach beyond our present topic, but they should help to clarify the logic of the difference between the vision of social vocation that we are studying and the traditional "Reformed" one.

If we reclaim the doctrine of vocation in the light of the practices and social vision that we are studying, then the specific ministry of the Christian banker or financier will be to find realistic, technically not utopian ways of implementing jubilee amnesty; there are people doing this. The Christian realtor or developer will find ways to house people according to need; there are people doing this. The Christian judge will open the court system to conflict resolution procedures, and resist the trend toward more and more litigation; this is being done. Technical vocational sphere expertise in each professional area will be needed not to reinforce but to undercut competently the claimed sovereignty of each sphere by planting signs of the new world in the ruins of the old. Baptism is one of those signs, and so is open housing. The Eucharist is one, but so is feeding the hungry. One is not more "real presence" than the other.

— *Body Politics*, 25–27

In a broader and deeper sense, the entire Christian community is sent into the world to "communicate a message and gather its hearers into communities." There should then not be one theology for professional missionaries and the agencies that send them abroad and another for ordinary Christians with no such call. What we do about social justice or about education should then be no less "missionary" than what we do about crossing linguistic or political borders and communicating our convictions to unbelievers.

— *For the Nations*, 7

SOCIAL CREATIVITY
IS A MINORITY FUNCTION

We have always been taught to understand the nature of power
in society so as to expect that the way to get useful things done
is to find a place at the command posts of the state. We have
suggested that the people in power are not so free or so strong
as they assume, that they are prisoners of the friends and the
promises they made in order to get into office. But an even
more basic observation is that they are not at the place in society where the greatest contribution can be made. The creativity
of the "pilot project" or of the critic is more significant for a
social change than is the coercive power that generalizes a new
idea. Those who are at the "top" of society are occupied largely
with the routine tasks of keeping in position and keeping balance in society. The dominant group in any society is the one
that provides its judges and lawyers, teachers and prelates —
their effort is largely committed to keeping things as they are.
This busyness of rulers with routine gives an exceptional leverage to the creative minority, sometimes because it can tip the
scales between two power blocs and sometimes because it can
pioneer a new idea. In every rapidly changing society a dispro-
portionate share of leadership is carried by cultural, racial, and
religious minorities.

What is said here about the cultural strength of the numerical and social minority could just as well be said with regard
to *political* strength. The freedom of the Christian, or of the
church, from needing to invest his or her best effort or the effort
of the Christian community, in obtaining the capacity to coerce
others, and exercising and holding on to this power, is precisely
the key to the creativity of the unique Christian mission in society. The rejection of violence appears to be social withdrawal
if we assume that violence is the key to all that happens in
society. But the logic shifts if we recognize that the number of
locks that can be opened with the key of violence is very limited. The renunciation of coercive violence is the prerequisite of

a genuinely creative social responsibility and to the exercise of those kinds of social power that are less self-defeating.

— The Royal Priesthood, 215

THE PREFERENTIAL OPTION
FOR THE POOR

Our Latino sisters and brothers have pressed upon us the notion of the "preferential option for the poor" in a way that has sometimes strained our semantic capacities. "Option" in English means you hold your future choices open, so the frequent recourse of transliteration gives a backward meaning. In Spanish and Portuguese the apparently cognate word means having taken sides. More recently others have assumed that the slogan means only that we should ask what is good for poor people, making it a question of political economy, or of social ethics, and have co-opted the phrase in favor of the paternalistic argument for the greater efficiency of trickle-down economies as a way to help more people get ahead.

It is rhetorically silly to argue about what is the one right meaning of a slogan that has gone public. What we should argue about is the originally valid substance behind it. The clearer and in my mind the most adequate paraphrase, one which has also gone public, but which I first heard used by José Míguez Bonino, one of my predecessors in this Wattson lectureship, speaks of "the epistemological privilege of the underdog."

This phrasing points us to the awareness that the first question is not who should be fed or who should govern, but whose picture of things is correct. We speak of an epistemological advantage. To see things from below is a truer way to see things as they are.

"As they are" in Spanish has two shades of meaning. *Como son* refers to things in their essence, what makes them what they are; *como están* takes account of the present state of things. Both levels of nuance apply. The underdog has a more accurate

picture of the present state of things, as well as of the underlying
character of the structures the rest of us profit from.

One reason to respect more the point of view of the underdogs is that there are more of them. If societies become more
authentically democratic, the underdogs will have more to say,
and the leaders they choose will have more authority. If societies fail to become more fair, it is "from below" that trouble
will come.

But for biblical faith the reason to privilege the view from
below is not population numbers nor political theory. It is that
below is the place from where God has repeatedly chosen to
see things, and from where God has called men and women to
participate in the enfranchisement. From Moses' mother leaving
him among the bulrushes to Jesus' parents fleeing Egypt, when
God advances his story line it begins with the vulnerable.

The *kenosis,* or humiliation, that God chooses as the path to
Lordship is not merely a mentality of self-abnegation or servanthood (although that too is of great weight, and will become
more weighty, as in a postmodern world we have to be more
intentional about our subjectivity). Nor is it merely a complex
of *moral* choices within a conflictive social history, though it
has to be that, too. Jesus' choice of the cross is the pinnacle
and prototype of that divine self-emptying, and it has been followed by the Romeros and the Kings and Gandhis who have
retrieved and reincarnated that suffering servant vision for our
century. Yet it is more than the ethos. Underlying the ethos, as
I said at the outset, is an epistemology, or an insight. We are
called to *see* a different reality; to *see through* what people at
the top of our society call "realism." That ethos, and that spirituality, and that insight, can also sometimes be implemented,
without all the pathos of literal martyrdom, in the ordinari-
ness of life, as Paul did when he said that he rejoiced that
God's treasure had been entrusted to him in earthenware ves-
sels, "to show that the transcendent power belongs to God, and
not to me."

The people of God will be moving toward the unity God
seeks when and as we see our Eucharist as a locus and focus of

sharing bread with the hungry. Our espousing "the view from below" will become real as we see our baptism creating the solidarity which Paul called a "new creation," bonding insiders and outsiders in one family. That new household is called to accept being at the bottom of the heap as the place from which to see how things really are.   — "On Christian Unity," 175–76

Sources
Works by John Howard Yoder

Body Politics: Five Practices of the Christian Community before the Watching World. Scottdale, Pa.: Herald Press, 1992.

Christian Attitudes to War, Peace, and Revolution. Edited by Theodore J. Koontz and Andy Alexis-Baker. Grand Rapids, Mich.: Brazos Press, 2009.

The Christian Witness to the State. Institute of Mennonite Studies Series 3. Newton, Kans.: Faith and Life Press, 1977. First published in 1964.

Discipleship as Political Responsibility. Translated by Timothy J. Geddart. Scottdale, Pa.: Herald Press, 2003. First published as *Nachfolge Christi als Gestalt politischer Verantwortung.* Basel: Agape Verlag, 1964.

The Ecumenical Movement and the Faithful Church. Focal Pamphlet Series no. 3. Scottdale, Pa.: Mennonite Publishing House, 1958.

For the Nations: Essays Public and Evangelical. Grand Rapids, Mich.: Eerdmans, 1997.

He Came Preaching Peace. Scottdale, Pa.: Herald Press, 1985. Reprinted by Wipf and Stock, 1998.

The Jewish-Christian Schism Revisited. Radical Traditions Series. Edited by Michael G. Cartwright and Peter Ochs. Grand Rapids, Mich.: Eerdmans, 2003.

Nevertheless: Varieties of Religious Pacifism. Rev. ed. Scottdale, Pa.: Herald Press, 1992. First published in 1971.

Nonviolence: A Brief History — The Warsaw Lectures. Edited by Paul Martens, Matthew Porter, and Myles Werntz. Waco, Tex.: Baylor University Press, 2010.

"On Christian Unity: The Way from Below." *Pro Ecclesia* 9, no. 2 (2000): 165–83.

"On the Meaning of Christmas." *Concern* 16 (November 1968): 14–19.

The Original Revolution: Essays on Christian Pacifism. Scottdale, Pa.: Herald Press, 2003. First published in 1971.

The Politics of Jesus: Vicit Agnus Noster. 2nd ed. Grand Rapids, Mich.: Eerdmans, 1994. First published in 1972.

Preface to Theology: Christology and Theological Method. Edited by Stanley Hauerwas and Alex Sider. Grand Rapids, Mich.: Brazos, 2002.

The Priestly Kingdom: Social Ethics as Gospel. Notre Dame, Ind.: University of Notre Dame Press, 1984.

The Royal Priesthood: Essays Ecclesiological and Ecumenical. Ed. Michael G. Cartwright. Scottdale, Pa.: Herald Press, 1998. First published by Eerdmans in 1994.

"A Study in the Doctrine of the Work of Christ." Unpublished lecture for American Mennonite students in Europe at a seminar in Domburg, Netherlands. April 27, 1954.

To Hear the Word. Eugene, Ore.: Wipf and Stock, 2001.

The War of the Lamb: The Ethics of Nonviolence and Peacemaking. Edited by Glen Stassen, Mark Thiessen Nation, and Matt Hamsher. Grand Rapids, Mich.: Brazos, 2009.

What Would You Do? A Serious Answer to a Standard Question. Expanded ed. Scottdale, Pa.: Herald Press, 1992. First published in 1983.

When War Is Unjust: Being Honest in Just-War Thinking. 2nd. ed. Maryknoll, N.Y.: Orbis, 1996. First published by Augsburg Publishing House in 1984.

MODERN SPIRITUAL MASTERS
Robert Ellsberg, Series Editor

This series introduces the essential writing and vision of some of the great spiritual teachers of our time. While many of these figures are rooted in long-established traditions of spirituality, others have charted new, untested paths. In each case, however, they have engaged in a spiritual journey shaped by the challenges and concerns of our age. Together with the saints and witnesses of previous centuries, these modern spiritual masters may serve as guides and companions to a new generation of seekers.

Already published:

Flannery O'Connor (edited by Robert Ellsberg)
Clarence Jordan (edited by Joyce Hollyday)
G. K. Chesterton (edited by William Griffin)
Alfred Delp, S.J. (introduction by Thomas Merton)
Bede Griffiths (edited by Thomas Matus)
Karl Rahner (edited by Philip Endean)
Pedro Arrupe (edited by Kevin F. Burke, S.J.)
Sadhu Sundar Singh (edited by Charles E. Moore)
Romano Guardini (edited by Robert A. Krieg)
Albert Schweitzer (edited by James Brabazon)
Caryll Houselander (edited by Wendy M. Wright)
Brother Roger of Taizé (edited by Marcello Fidanzio)
Dorothee Soelle (edited by Dianne L. Oliver)
Leo Tolstoy (edited by Charles E. Moore)
Howard Thurman (edited by Luther E. Smith, Jr.)
Swami Abhishiktananda (edited by Shirley du Boulay)
Carlo Carretto (edited by Robert Ellsberg)
Pope John XXIII (edited by Jean Maalouf)
Modern Spiritual Masters (edited by Robert Ellsberg)
Jean Vanier (edited by Carolyn Whitney-Brown)
The Dalai Lama (edited by Thomas A. Forsthoefel)
Catherine de Hueck Doherty (edited by
    David Meconi, S.J.)
Dom Helder Camara (edited by Francis McDonagh)
Daniel Berrigan (edited by John Dear)
Etty Hillesum (edited by Annemarie S. Kidder)
Virgilio Elizondo (edited by Timothy Matovina)
Yves Congar (edited by Paul Lakeland)
Metropolitan Anthony of Sourozh (edited by
    Gillian Crow)
David Steindl-Rast (edited by Clare Hallward)
Frank Sheed and Maisie Ward (edited by David Meconi)
Abraham Joshua Heschel (edited by Susannah Heschel)